THE FIRST READING AND WRITING BOOK

THE FIRST READING AND WRITING BOOK

Margaret Hooton

HEINEMANN
LONDON

Heinemann Educational Books Ltd
22 Bedford Square, London WC1B 3HH
London Edinburgh Melbourne Auckland
Hong Kong Singapore Kuala Lumpur New Delhi
Ibadan Nairobi Johannesburg Kingston
Exeter (NH) Port of Spain

First published by Shepheard-Walwyn (Publishers) Ltd 1976
Reprinted 1976
First published by Heinemann Educational Books 1977
Reprinted 1978, 1979, 1981, 1983

ISBN 0 435 01343 2

The First Reading and Writing Scheme

comprising
The First Reading and Writing Book
ISBN (hardback) 0 435 01342 4
ISBN (paperback)* 0 435 01343 2

The Practice Book*
ISBN 0 435 01344 0

The Dictionary*
ISBN 0 435 01345 9

The Wallcharts*
ISBN 0 435 01346 7

PACK
comprising one copy of starred items above
ISBN 0 435 01347 5

Printed in Hong Kong by
Dah Hua Printing Press Co Ltd.

CONTENTS

INTRODUCTION

There is no one method which will convey to all children all they need to know about reading and writing. Often it is difficult for parents and teachers to decide which of the available methods they should follow, and this must vary from child to child. There are, nonetheless, certain facts and conventions which it is helpful for a child to understand. The basis of language lies in the sounds that we make, for these are what the written words represent. The number of different sounds which must be recognized from what is written may seem overwhelming, but if they are presented simply and methodically confidence will be established from the beginning.

This book sets out an orderly presentation of basic concepts. A simple way of forming each letter and a basic sound it represents are given together. From this twofold basis of writing and reading recognition of letters, words and phrases quickly grows. It is clear that no ready grasp of reading can take place unless the sounds represented by some groups of letters can be recognized at sight—'the' is an example. For this reason 'sight words' are introduced at convenient places for the children to say and write. This they readily do by imitation, and so learn that the same written letters need not always have the same sounds.

Children love to learn. They love an orderly progression, going from step to step. They love to imitate. We can make use of these aptitudes to start them off in such a way that the pleasure of reading is soon discovered. When reading and writing spring from a good foundation spelling and comprehension follow more easily. Practice in the orderly use of his mind helps a child to establish orderly behaviour, and this is reflected in his other activities.

Some points observed

The sounds of the letters are used first, and when these are established, the names are introduced as well.

The lower-case form of the letters is used first, and the upper case (capital) form given when the two will not be confused.

The short vowels are introduced at the beginning. They occur so frequently that their recognition gives immediate pleasure and confidence. Studies have shown that 45 per cent of words are made up of a pattern consisting of a short vowel at the beginning or in the middle of a word or syllable.[1] The simple sounds of the consonants follow, the sound which has been chosen for each letter is that most frequently used in order to give immediate use and success (see page 5).

The letters are not given in their alphabetical order, but the alphabet is constantly presented with the known letters picked out so that their place becomes familiar.

The names of the objects are not written on the pages of illustrations. The initial sound can thus be emphasized, and the child is not confused by letters or sounds not yet presented.

The presentation of 'b' and 'd' is kept well separated to avoid a frequent source of uncertainty.

To help with writing, frequently occurring consonants are presented in families of related shapes:

the circle and straight line letters: c t p s b g l
the 'h' family: h n m r
the diagonal family: v w y x z.

It has been found that by grouping the shapes, particularly with the use of templates, children find the task of learning to write so many forms more comprehensible. Then with practice, the technical skill of writing requires much less effort and the child is left free to set down what he wants to express.

Proportion and the form of the letter, and its relationship to the line, is stressed to give a sound foundation from which a legible handwriting can be developed. The quality of writing is important since through it a child may be taught care and accuracy.

The concepts presented in this book provide a basis from which further instruction in reading can proceed, using whatever methods or schemes are available. Although knowledge of more complex sounds and words has yet to be added, the foundations will have been laid for knowing why a word says what it does.

Variations in dialect or pronunciation of the letters are of little importance in this approach as the sound is taken either from the child's pronunciation of that sound in a word, or from the teacher's if the child's needs clarification or correction. It has been found that speech defects markedly diminish when this way is followed.

[1] See for example, Edith Potter, 'Six Types of Syllables to Simplify your Spelling and Word Attack', Edith Potter Publications, 1955, New York.

GENERAL GUIDANCE

The Child's Attitudes

It is of great help to the child if, from the very beginning, he is encouraged to establish positive attitudes and habits towards all the work connected with reading and writing. Occasionally in conversation you can remind him, by asking appropriate questions, of the reasons for wanting to read. Often the desire to read is strong, sometimes it is weak, and sometimes it is quite negative. The desire to read may be sparked off and encouraged by reading good stories as often as possible. Having a variety of books available for the child to look at is a great help. The quality of these books, and their standard of printing and illustration, should be as high as possible.

The child will copy the way in which the person teaching him handles books, and careful handling will encourage a respect for them. Help him to turn pages carefully and to have clean hands. Respect also grows if the quality of the stories is high. We are fortunate at the moment in having available a wealth of stories, myths and legends from many cultures, often attractively presented. Read to him as much as possible from the great collections of fairy tales, nursery rhymes, adventure stories and stories of great men and women. Give him an indication of the riches waiting for him when he can read for himself.

The child's attitude to the person teaching him is also important. Mutual respect and recognition of the roles of teacher and pupil (even when the parent is acting as teacher) eases the work on both sides.

Attention

The teacher's attention is vital. If the person teaching keeps in mind the word or sentence or subject under consideration, the child picks it up much more easily. Likewise, if the teacher's mind wanders the child's mind is likely to wander as well. Many difficulties arise because a child has got into the habit of not listening and not looking. Exercises to cultivate the child's attention can take the form of games. Some suggestions for these can be found on page 131.

Another way to encourage good use of the senses is by asking spot questions:

'What was the sky like when you were coming to school this morning?'
'Did you notice any birds?'
'What sounds can you hear now?'

You will have, of course, to suit the questions to locality and circumstances:

'What did you notice about the smell of things after that rain?'

To settle a distracted child (or class) get him to listen, first to the smallest sounds within the room, then to the farthest sounds outside it. Ask the child to listen to the sound of his own voice. It is important to develop this habit of listening, as otherwise he will sound out a word perfectly but, forgetting to listen, will not have any idea of what he has just said. He will rely on hearing his teacher's voice sounding out the word. This is acceptable at first, but gradually you should encourage the child to listen to his *own* voice. Seeing and hearing together help to establish knowledge of the words. At the beginning also encourage the use of the sense of touch by providing cardboard templates or wooden letters, and mounted sandpaper letters (see page 135 for some advice on how to make these).

In writing, when he has achieved a shape tell the child to 'teach his hand how to do it'. Get him to close his eyes and feel what his hand or arm is doing. Suggest that he listen to the pencil on the paper or the chalk on the blackboard, and encourage him to look at the point of the pencil where it is writing on the paper so that he actually sees the shapes he is making. Helpful self-correction will often follow this practice.

From time to time it is good to change the places of seating, so that fixed habits of seeing and hearing do not creep in.

Confidence

Praise is the teacher's most valuable tool, but it should be used carefully. Do not praise falsely or give credit for effort of inadequate standard.

Any child can do something praiseworthy—start at that point for each child you teach. Self-respect is thus nurtured and in this atmosphere learning can take place.

Establish confidence at every step. When success at any point is achieved, establish it by repetition before proceeding to the next point. This is basic to successful learning.

Establish the sound of a letter,
the sound of a syllable,
the sound of a word,
the sound of a sentence,
so that the groundwork is secure.

When he is writing, ask the child to select the best form from his own row of letters and to repeat this form until he himself is satisfied.

Revision helps to establish confidence. Although it is tempting to keep forging ahead, from time to time rest, and look to see that everything is well established. For example, suppose one wished to revise the shape of a known letter 'p':

Show the child a good example of the letter (you could use one of the examples in this book);
Ask him to close his eyes and see it in his mind;
Tell him to open his eyes and look at the example again;
Ask him to close his eyes and see it in his mind again;
Opening his eyes, he should write what he saw in his mind.
Then he can teach his hand and fingers how to form exactly the shape he saw.

Be quick to pick up an area of confusion. In a class, one child showing confusion will be an indication that probably others are similarly confused. It will do no harm to take an entire lesson to clear whatever is causing the confusion, as the repetition will also serve as a reinforcement for those who have already understood.

Imitation

Use this powerful instrument of learning lavishly. Do not forget that pupils imitate their teacher's attitudes, movements, habits, voice and tastes. Use this to advantage. Let your own enjoyment of the sounds and shapes of the letters be evident, and that also will be imitated by the child and linked with reading and writing.

Concerning reading specifically, imitation of good flowing reading is important. Phrasing and intonation are easily taught early in reading. Fluency can be explained by the image of a river flowing. Let the child imitate your voice speaking known sentences. Let him act out sentences, speaking naturally as he acts. The ease which comes with fluency will promote understanding of what is read.

Ensure that even the first simple sentences are understood, as often, to begin with, the child does not connect the written word with meaning; for example:

Sentence: The cat is black.
Questions: What is black?
What colour is the cat?
Is the cat pink?

Practise reading together very softly, very loudly, sadly, happily and so on, and the stage of the stilted 'The—cat—sat—on—the—mat' will be minimal.

Help

Homework is of great value to the child. Once they know this most parents will cooperate with and respect a teacher who sets it regularly and expects it to be well done. Teachers should ask parents to help establish the habit of homework as early as possible. Homework should be of reasonable duration. It is easiest and of most use if done at a regular time, and should reinforce the day's work, setting a confident stage for the next step.

In a group, it will be seen that at certain points particular children can help each other to their mutual benefit. Sometimes they may work completely together, with one taking the part of teacher, and then reversing roles. They can give each other exercises and games. Often a child's perceptive assessment of why another is having difficulty is most helpful to their teacher.

Surroundings

Try to ensure that the room in which the child is taught is tidy and uncluttered. A classroom should be simple, light and comfortably taken in at a glance. This makes it easier for a child to see and hear essential instructions. A few charts or examples concerning what is being studied are useful for reinforcement or reference, and old ones are best removed. For restfulness, one or two pictures of fine quality and some fresh flowers or leaves help keep the feeling in a room light. Over-stimulation from too many sources is confusing for children and particularly so for those with any learning difficulty.

Further experience

It is recommended that reading-books of a general nature are presented as soon as the child has mastered enough to tackle them without becoming discouraged. The more widely he reads, the keener and more confident he will become. Phonically structured readers such as the 'Bangers and Mash' series (Longman) and 'The Royal Road Readers' (Chatto and Windus Educational) and those published under 'The Language Project' directed by Dr J. M. Morris give useful practice. Success with such readers gives confidence to try others.

It goes without saying that children should be read to from an early age. Choose a wide variety of nursery rhymes, stories, poems and fairy-tales. Favourites will emerge and mutual enjoyment will do much to foster a love of books and reading. In the process many of the conventions of reading will be absorbed.

Children do *not* necessarily have to identify with what they are reading. A certain amount of practice in reading about familiar situations is useful. But as a child is given more and more of the tools of reading he will come to know the delight of discovering that he can make sense out of printed words even when they are describing events in time and space much greater than those within his own limited experience. He will enjoy experimenting with words in much the same way as he enjoys experimenting with numbers.

HOW TO USE THIS BOOK

The approach given in this book is one which any parent or teacher may follow. The ideas given may be expanded into whole lessons. Some of the concepts will be quickly grasped and others will need much expansion and repetition. For individual teaching, or very small groups, the pages in the book will be sufficient for demonstration. For a classroom, wall charts are available.

The form of the book is based on the orderly presentation of basic concepts. Some of these may at first sight appear too obvious to be worth stating, but it is astonishing how many children have had their progress severely retarded because of confusion about a small but vital fact. Eventually all these concepts must be understood. Be prepared to go very slowly at first, making sure these simple points are really comprehended. If a child appears to be having difficulty it is well worth systematically checking whether or not he has understood the basic concepts, and going over them again where he is in doubt. When it is necessary to explain an idea again to slower learners, children who have grasped it quickly can do extra practice.

Throughout this book, which is an *introduction* to reading, each letter is given just one sound, and this may be referred to as the *simple sound* for that letter. This gives a firm basis from which to work. It also gives hope to those children who feel there is an infinite number of sounds to master and who have become discouraged at the idea. Children will ask about other sounds a letter might have, for instance the sound of 'a' in aunt, the sound of 'c' in ice, and then it can be explained that when letters are combined with other letters their sounds change, and that you will help them with that in due course. To begin with, and to get started, use the *simple sounds* and then the more complex ones will be easy when they are needed. When introducing a new letter refer to it at first by its simple sound, and not by its name.

Many children in difficulty will be found to be unsure of the sounds of letters. Do not hesitate to start at the beginning by checking every sound, remembering that praise and patience are two of your most valuable aids. Confusion between the sounds and names of letters and between capital and lower-case versions of letters is very common (calling them 'big' and 'small' is not accurate and can lead to difficulties). If these points are all dealt with slowly and carefully in the order presented, the troubles will soon be cleared away and the ensuing confidence will allow the child to approach one by one a hitherto frightening assortment of letters.

No word is presented for reading or writing which cannot be worked out by sound from what has already been taught in a previous lesson, or which has not been learnt as a 'sight' word. But do not inhibit an adventurous reading and writing vocabulary, which can be noted for use in his personal dictionary (see page 68). Sight words and other important concepts when first introduced are underlined in red. The progression is logical and immediately comprehensible to both the teacher and the child.

This approach has been used successfully for people with learning difficulties irrespective of age, and for remedial work with immigrant, dyslexic, maladjusted and partially-sighted children.

In the text of the book, some of the sentences are printed in **bold type.** These are suggestions for what to say to the child. The rest of the book, printed in ordinary type, is addressed to the parent or teacher and is designed to help make the lessons meaningful and interesting. For example (from page 9):

'**When we read a book we always start on the page at the beginning of the book.**

'Demonstrate "beginning" and "end" of books.'

The instructions for teaching the letter 'a' are given in full, including practices, drills, and the use of simple aids. Similar procedures should be followed as each letter is introduced. The exercises given may be regarded as suggestions on which to base repetitions and variations, suited to the particular needs of the child or children being taught.

Instructions and patterns for making the aids are to be found at the end of the book. *These should be prepared before starting the lessons.* In particular, see that the letter templates are ready. Simply paste pages onto firm card or plywood, and cut them out carefully. The charts referred to in the text are also printed on page 18, and at the end of the book.

Games to reinforce points being taught are given in the course of the book. Other exercises and games to train the senses will be found on page 131. The pictures may be coloured in as sounds are mastered.

ORDER OF PRESENTATION

CONCEPTS OF SPACE

Certain simple concepts of space, although so obvious to us that we take them for granted, are not necessarily clear to all children unless they are explained and demonstrated. It is of great importance that the following terms are thoroughly understood, as with them we establish the order of things we are dealing with:

beginning	—	end
right	—	left
top	—	bottom
first	—	last
forwards	—	backwards
up	—	down
in	—	out
inside	—	outside
in front	—	behind

With these ideas firmly in place children are much less likely to sound letters in the wrong order, to write backwards or change the places of letters when spelling. Much poor reading and spelling comes about simply because the clear idea of orderly progression has not been laid down initially.

Games and competitions using the child's whole body in relation to space and things around him are useful here. For example: moving in given directions; walking on lines; stepping on alternate squares on the floor; following instructions for moving under, over, on to objects, etc.

Take all kinds and sizes of books and go over the following ideas together.

When we read a book we always start on the page at the <u>beginning</u> of the book.

Demonstrate 'beginning' and 'end' of books.

The concept of right and left may take a long time to instil but make a start. If you have a class or a group of children take a lesson on 'left' and 'right', and refer to it often as opportunities arise during singing, physical education, art work and other lessons. For a mother teaching a child, many opportunities will arise naturally during the day, such as when dressing, at mealtimes and out walking.

Put a sticky label on child's left hand, explaining that when the left hand is referred to, it is the labelled hand, and the right is unlabelled.

Using a book, indicate clearly by pointing to and handling the pages, the following terms.

We read the left-hand page before we read the right-hand page.

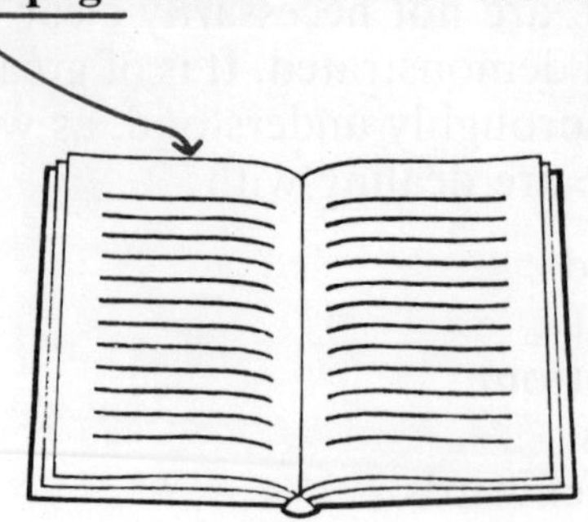

We start to read at the top of the page

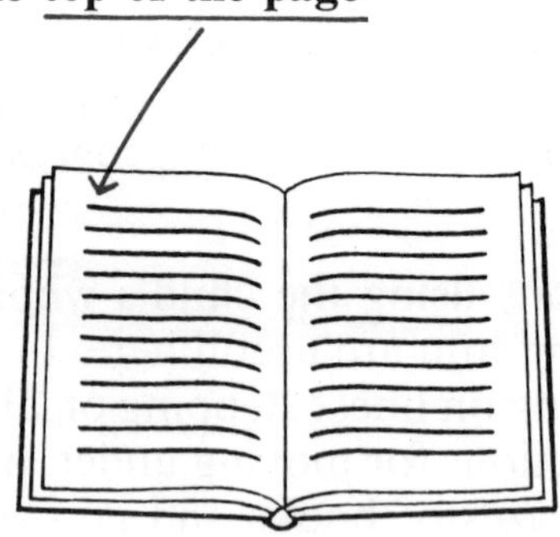

and read every line down to the bottom.

Check that 'line' is understood. Find many examples of 'top' and 'bottom' (tins, boxes, doors, windows, etc) interspersing with tops and bottoms of pages.

The beginning of the line is at the left-hand side of the page.
This is how we would read two pages. Trace the order of the words with your finger as you would read them.

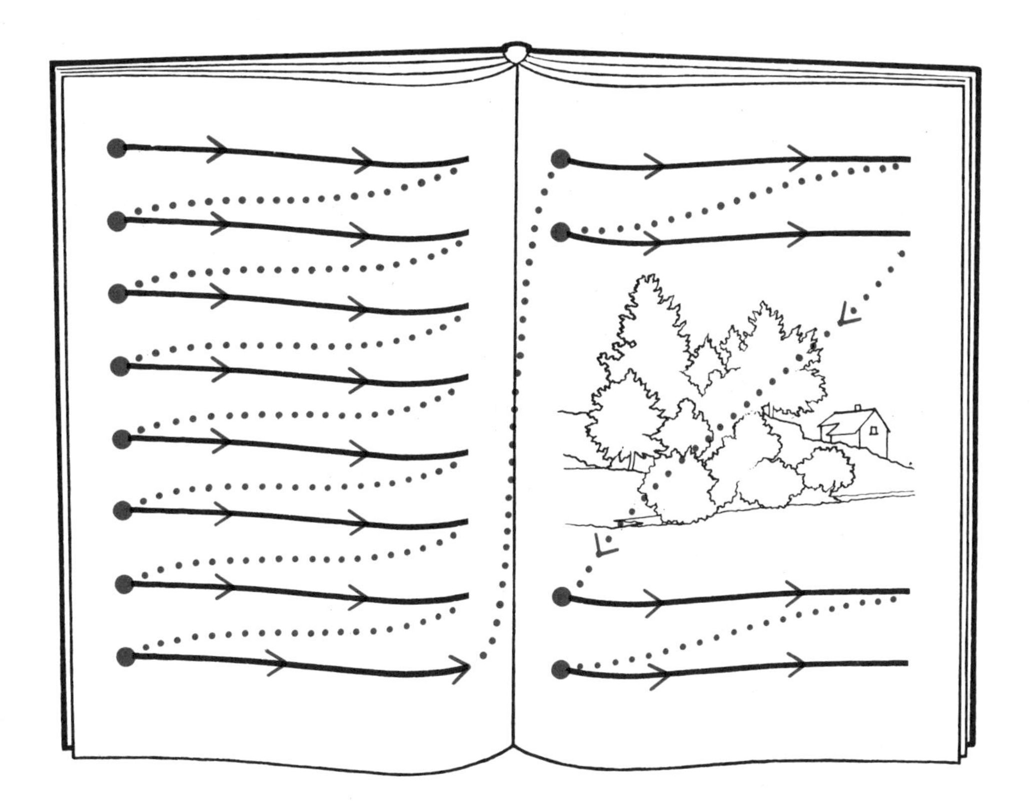

A way to teach some of these terms is to draw a row of three objects on the blackboard or on a piece of paper, using whatever is of interest to the child or class at the moment—buses, trees, etc. For example:

Here is a row of bells.

Point as you speak, going from left to right.

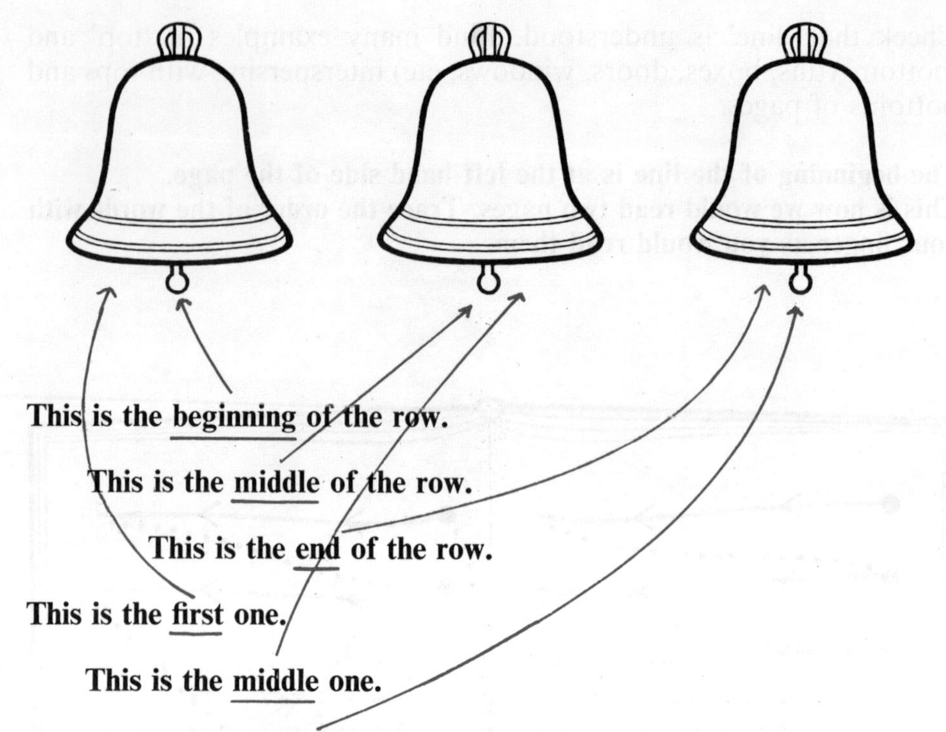

Take all kinds of examples of beginning, middle, end; first, middle, last. Finish with an example of a word:

Here is a word made up of letters:

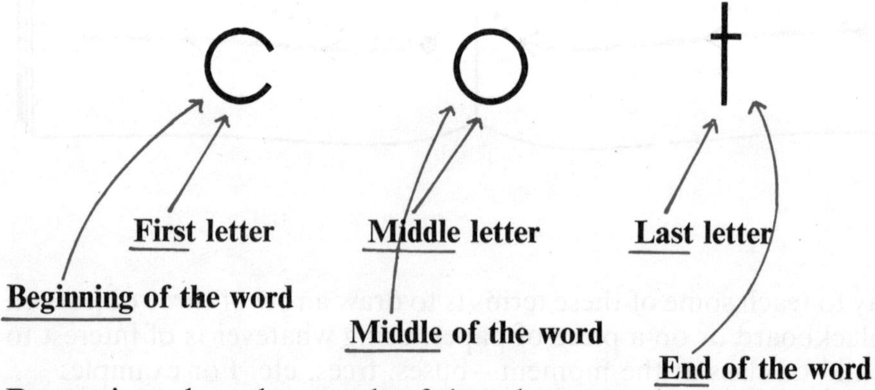

Do not introduce the sounds of these letters at the moment, just concentrate on the order and the terms used, as an example of the way letters are arranged.

INTRODUCTION TO WRITING

To prepare hand and eye for writing and reading, give plenty of practice in drawing the basic shapes involved in the formation of letters. These shapes are simply straight lines and circles, and if from the beginning they are started in the appropriate place and drawn in proportion, many possible later difficulties will be avoided.

Straight Lines
Give practice in drawing lines on the blackboard or pieces of paper, drawing from top left to top right, and so on down to the bottom.

Have plenty of prepared paper with large dots at starting and finishing points.

Practise lines of different colours, different thicknesses, and finally different shapes, but *all* must start at the top left and proceed systematically.

Note: The terms horizontal and vertical may be omitted for very young children but on the whole it is found that they enjoy them.

These are horizontal lines. Draw some just like them, starting at the left at the top of the page.

Red dots are used from now on to indicate where to begin writing.

Next let the child practise on lined paper in an exercise book. The kind which has a red line margin down the left hand side is best. It is always best to demonstrate clearly first what is to be done, as the spoken instruction is often mis-heard or misunderstood.

It is well worth developing the routine of beginning each writing and reading session with drawing lines from left to right. Something well known but needing care brings the child's mind to rest on the work before him. Vary your instructions and make the exercise enjoyable.

For example:

Let's do it fast.
Let's do it slowly.
Now press heavily.

Press very lightly.
Listen to your pencil on the paper (or the chalk on the blackboard).
Watch the point of your pencil carefully.

While the child is writing, give reminders such as:

Where is the beginning?
Where is the end?
Where is the middle?

Sometimes introduce the alternative terms—first, middle, last.

Lines going along, as we have been doing them, are called horizontal lines.

Point out all the things you can think of which are in the form of horizontal lines—window ledges, door sills, edges of tables, etc.

As well as horizontal lines, there are lines which go up and down. These are called vertical lines.

Find examples.

Let us make all kinds of vertical lines—thick, thin, tall, short, fast, slow, heavy, light.

Prepare, or have cyclostyled, pages of dots that can be joined by vertical lines.
Make sure that the children always draw the lines from top to bottom.

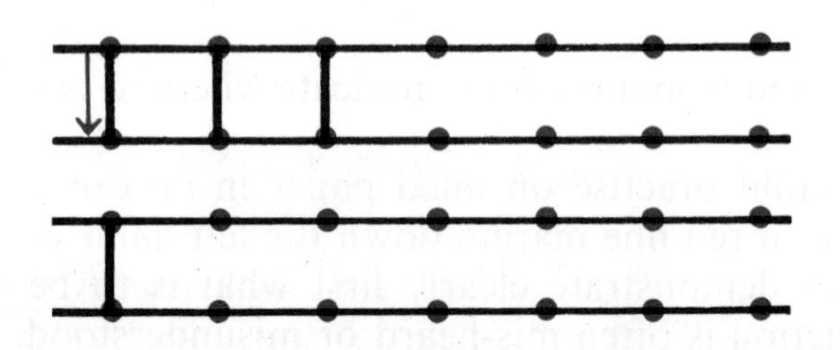

Circles

Letters are made up of straight lines and circles, so now that you are good at lines, let's try circles.

Take a lesson, which may extend over a long period, on the ideas of 'round', 'circle' and 'ring' and collect many pictures. These can be drawn or cut out or made into a collage, individually or as a class. Make cardboard or wooden templates of different sizes, some circles, some hollow rings. Children will be fascinated if you show them how a pair of compasses is used.

A circle is easy to draw, but remember to make it quite round, just like a wheel.

It is very important when you make the circle for writing to start it at the right place.

This is at about the place where 2 is on the face of a clock. (Show it on a clock.) **Follow the direction of the red arrow.**

You will see for yourself why this is so when we begin to make letters.

Establishing the habit of starting the circles at the 2 o'clock point means that the letters 'a', 'd', 'g' and 'q' will always be well joined across the top. The common confusion between 'u' and 'a' in both reading and spelling is less likely to occur. This 2 o'clock point is also the place to start 'c', 's' and 'f' and is the finishing point for 'r'. See that it is well practised.

Get the children to make many circles, preferably on the blackboard or on big pieces of paper, using many colours and sizes. When the circles are reasonably round and always started in the correct place, put them between lines, touching both the top and bottom lines. When proficiently done, transfer to books with lines. Let this take several lessons, repeating and expanding the instructions.

For making letters, we need two lengths of vertical straight lines—small ones and tall ones. The tall ones are twice as high as the small ones.

The small ones are the same height as the circles.

Tall lines and small lines *all* start at the *top*.

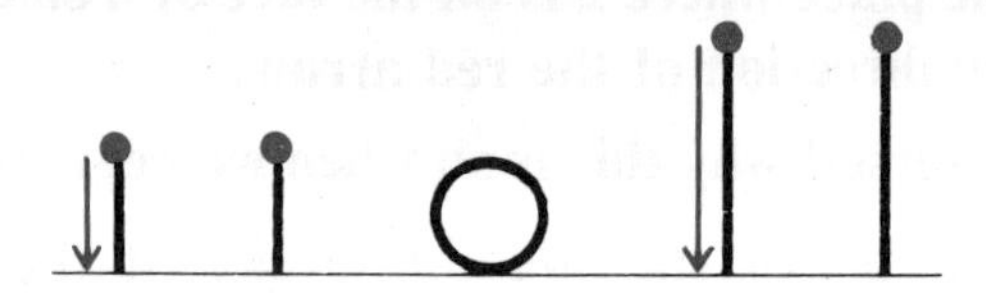

Take much practice of small and tall lines in various combinations, checking to see that the small lines are half the height of the tall. Demonstrate with the template of the tall line and two small lines.

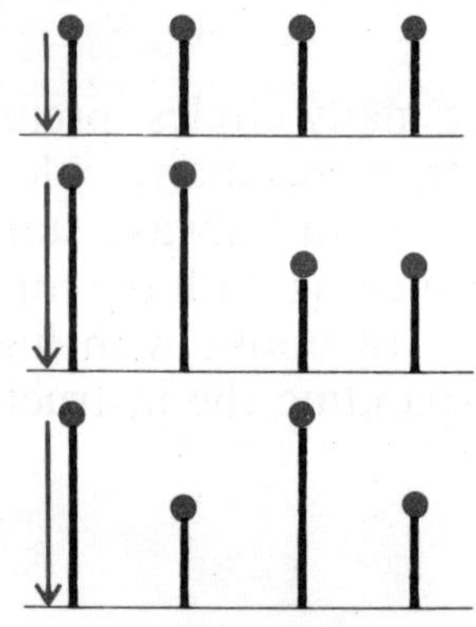

Daily practice may now consist of horizontal lines of various kinds:

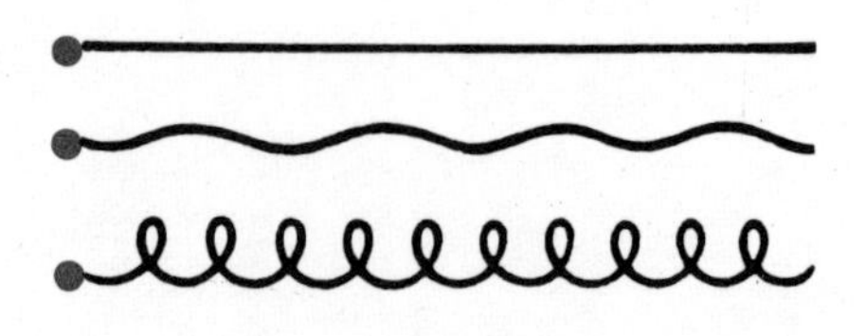

as well as vertical lines and circles. See that the circle and the small vertical line are of the same height and the tall vertical line twice that height. Let the children practise on blackboards or on large pieces of paper. It does not matter what size of line they start with as long as the proportion of small to tall is understood and correct. See that the circles always start at the right place.

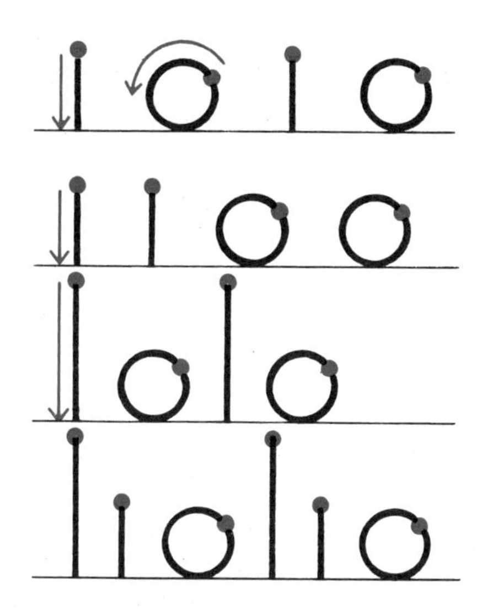

The children will invent their own patterns.

a b c d e f

g h i j k l

m n o p q r

s t u v w x

y z

THE ALPHABET

'The Alphabet' is the name we give to a collection of all the letters.

Here are all the letters.

These are called lower case letters.

There are 26 letters.

Each letter has a sound.

Each letter has a name also, but to begin with we shall use only the sound, as blending the sounds together helps us to find the sounds of words, and this is an important part of reading. So now we shall learn the sound of each of the letters.

Listening games such as those mentioned on pages 133 and 134 are a useful preliminary to what follows.
It is very useful to have a big copy of the chart on page 18 (available through the publishers) on the wall, at eye level and where it will be often seen. Appropriate pictures can be drawn or pasted on.

THE FIVE VOWELS

abcdefghijklmnopqrst uvwxyz

The letters in red are called the <u>vowels</u> and they appear so often that we shall find one or more of them in every word we see.

At this point concentrate on the shape only, not the sound of the letters.

So if we write and sound the vowels well, we are making an excellent beginning with reading.

Using the page opposite let the children find similar shapes.

How many of this shape— a **—can you see?**

How many of this shape— e **—can you see?**

How many of this shape— i **—can you see?**

How many of this shape— o **—can you see?**

How many of this shape— u **—can you see?**

abcdefghijklmnopqrstuvwxyz

a

The first vowel we shall learn is a

Find it in the alphabet chart (page 18, or the wallchart).

The sound of it is 'a' as you can hear it at the beginning of (the teacher here speaks very slowly and clearly, listening to her own voice, as children will pick up from this how to listen to their own voices):

apple, ants, at, alphabet, attic,
am, arrow, anchor, axe.

The objects illustrated on the opposite page all begin with the sound of this letter. The words underlined above are the ones to use, so check that the axe is identified as an axe, not as a chopper, and that the ants are ants, not insects! Get the children to repeat the names of the things, listening to their own voices and associating the sound at the beginning of the word with the symbol at the top of the page.

Follow this routine with each letter as it is presented. The words needed will be underlined in the list given for the initial sound. They are not printed on the illustrated page as irregular spelling can cause confusion at this stage.

Sometimes we hear this sound at the beginning of a word, and sometimes in the middle.

Listen carefully to these words and you will hear the 'a' sound in the middle:
fat, man, cat, patch.

And in these long words:
battery, lantern, palace, contact.

Say the sound—'a'.

Think of some more words with the sound 'a' in them, listening carefully.

What are some names beginning with this sound? . . . Ann, Alan.

Find the appropriate picture and letter from the cards made from those printed at the back of this book (pages 143-151).

How is a written?

It is written with a circle and a small straight line.

Demonstrate with wooden or card templates, holding up the circle and applying the small straight line *on top of* the right-hand side (from child's point of view). Let children handle the templates of a circle, a small line and an a, comparing them and fitting them together. They may trace around the templates. Let them run their fingers round an a painted on sandpaper, saying 'a . . . a . . . .a' as heard at the beginning of apple.

Let them trace out a in a shallow sand tray (see page 135).

Have them make the shape in the air, saying the sound.

Write the letter with a finger on the table, saying the sound.

Make a big a in chalk on the floor or playground and let them walk on the shape, following the same direction as that in which it is to be written.

Make all kinds of funny as on the blackboard, fat ones, thin ones, as of all kinds of disproportion and mis-shape, letting the children see and formulate the mistakes. They love to pick out the errors and vigorously disclaim any possibility of their making any such mistake.

On large pieces of paper make a clear a that the children can trace over with different colours of crayon.

Finally let them start in a book with lines.

First make a line of circles, starting at the right place.

Next make a line of small straight lines.

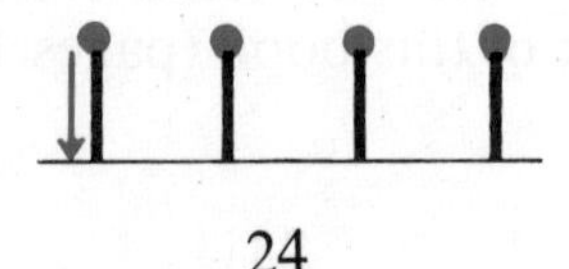

And now put them together starting with the circle, *round—up*—and—*down*. Say 'a' . . . . 'a' . . . . 'a' . . . . as you write.

abcdefghijklmnopqrstuvwxyz

The circle by itself is a letter.

Find it on the alphabet chart.

The sound of it is 'o' as in hot.

Say the sound—'o'.

Here are some words beginning with 'o':
orange, ostrich, office, on, off, omelette, octopus.

Look at the pictures and say their names.

Listen to the sound in the middle of these words:
pot, moss, blot, top.

Think of other words with the 'o' sound in the middle.

Here it is in longer words:
follow, upon, song, bother.

Here it is in names . . . Tom, Oliver, Polly.

You already know how to write it as it is a simple circle.

Go through practices as outlined for 'a' and finally let children write 'o' in their books, pointing out that it is the same size as the 'a'. Make sure that the circle is started in the right place, as this eases the formation of other letters.

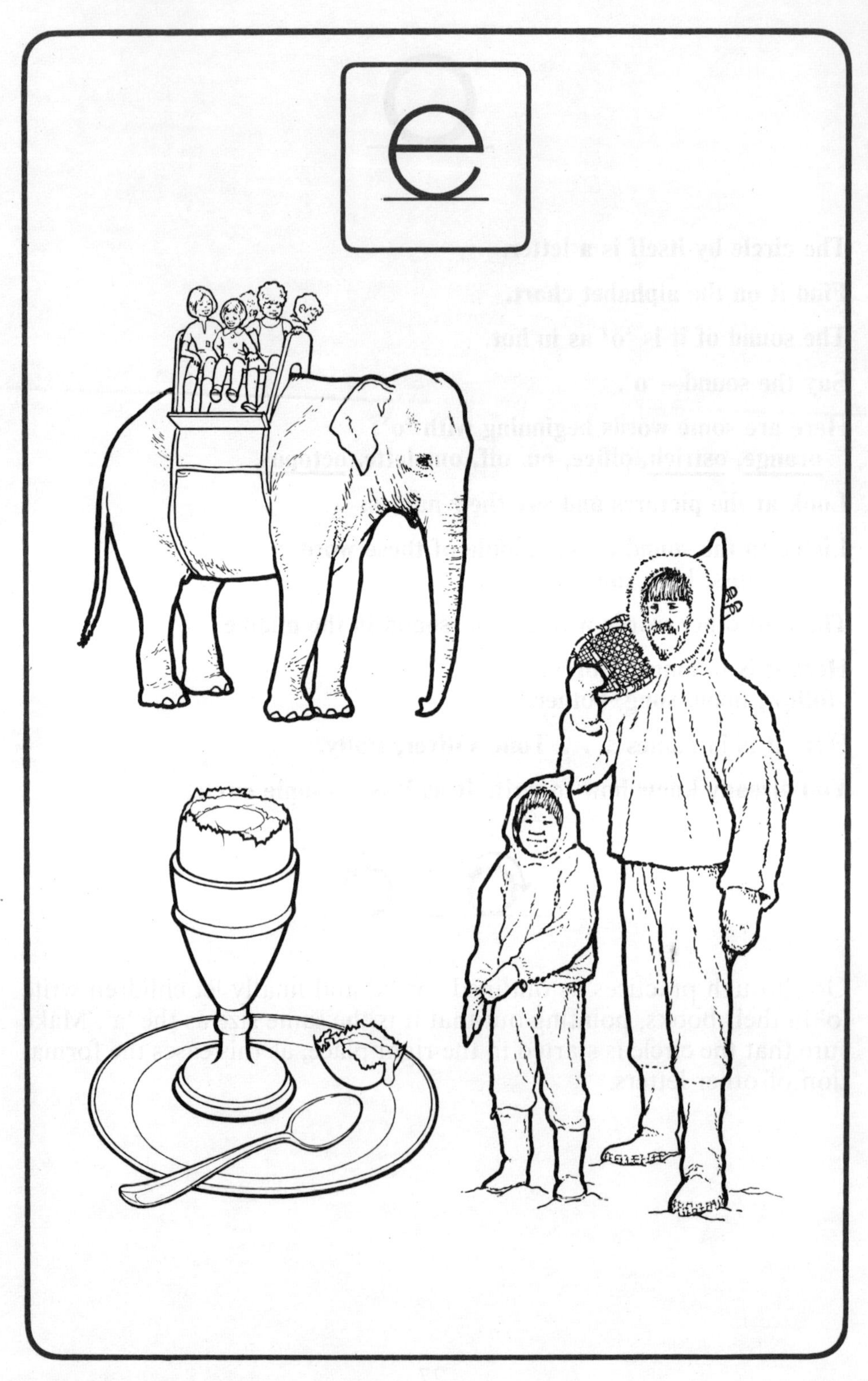

abcdefghijklmnopqrstuvwxyz

Where is this vowel on the alphabet chart?

The sound it has is ‘e’. Listen to the first sounds of these words:
egg, elephant, everybody, elbow, empty, expect, eskimo.

Look at the pictures and say their names.

Think of some more words beginning with ‘e’.

Listen to the ‘e’ in the middle of these words:
well, help, spelling, spent.

Say the sound—‘e’.

What are some names beginning with ‘e’?
Eric, Emily.

Take practice of straight horizontal lines and circles.

‘e’ is made of a straight line going across part of a circle.

Demonstrate with template o and e.

Now we shall make some ‘e’ shapes, starting at the beginning of the (horizontal) straight line, and going round a circle, stopping to leave a gap before we get up to the line.

See that the horizontal line lies half way between the lines on the paper.

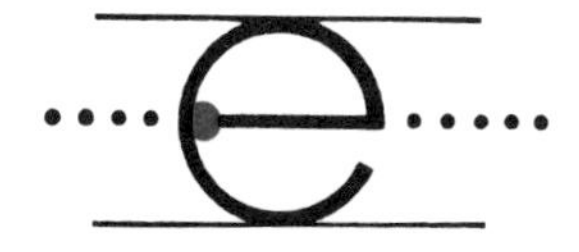

Use all the preparatory techniques as when introducing ‘a’.

Notice that e is the same size as a and o.

REVISION

Now we have three vowels—a, o, e.

Notice that they are *all the same size.* In practice check that the child is keeping them all the same size.

Call out 'a', 'o', 'e', and get children to write the appropriate letter, or a line of each.

Write down the vowel you hear at the beginning of this word—egg. Continue with apple, orange and so on.

Write down the vowel you hear in this word: pat, leg, lost, man, fox, send. Continue with other words.

Have games, sorting 'a', 'o' and 'e'. Print them in different colours and sizes on separate cards. Sort out words containing these vowels into different piles.

Draw chalk letters on floor or playground and have competitions for individual children, or team members, to jump onto the letter called out. Start by simply calling a letter; then make it more difficult by calling a word beginning with the wanted vowel; and finally by calling a word with the vowel in the middle.

For homework or practice tell children to find all the 'e's (or 'o's or 'a's on other nights) they can in newspapers and magazines. Cut them out and paste them on to suitable pages for class or individual use. In discussion of particular vowels found, concepts of large, small, fat, thin, tall, short can be spoken of. Children will bring 'a' as well as ɑ and this is a good time to accept this and point out where they will find it, and that its sound is exactly the same as the sound of ɑ.

abcdefghijklmnopqrstuvwxyz

A small straight line, when it has a dot above it, is the next of the vowels we are going to look at.

Where is it on the alphabet chart?

It is the sound 'i' at the beginning of ink, Indian, if, in, infant, insect, itchy, igloo.

Look at the pictures and say their names.

Say the sound—'i'.

If you listen carefully you will hear it in the middle of these words:
pig, lid, fit

and in these longer ones

lifting, picked, listening, fitting

and in these names

Elizabeth, Jill, Phillip.

Go over preliminary drills.

Practise writing a line of small vertical lines.

Then write a similar line but after each down line, put a dot above it.

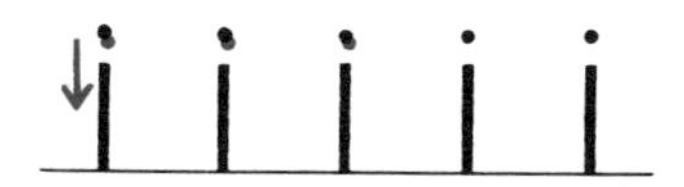

Practise a, o, e, i, in any of the ways previously suggested.

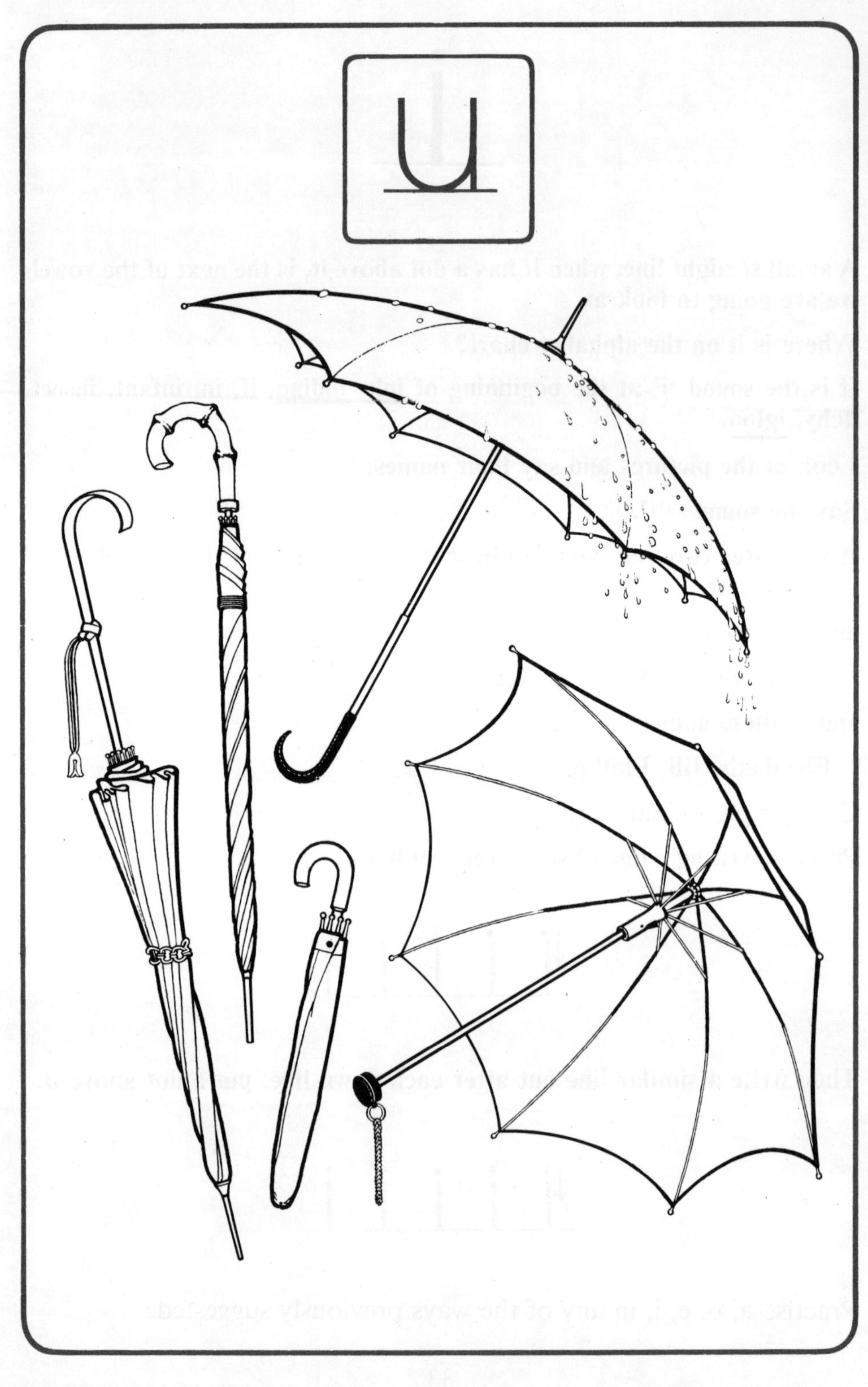

abcdefghijklmnopqrstuvwxyz

Do you remember that there are five vowels? We now know four of them: a, o, e, i, so there is just one left.

Which one is it?

Find it on the alphabet chart.

You can hear it at the beginning of:

up, under, umbrella, uncle.

Look at the pictures. Some umbrellas are up and some down.

You can hear it too, in the middle of these words:

cup, funny, mug, puddle.

Say the sound—'u'.

It is made up of two straight lines joined by part of a circle.

Show lines, circle, template of 'u'.

Go through all the introductory drills as for 'a' and finally let children write 'u' in books, pointing out that it is the same size as the 'a'.

REVISION

Revise knowledge of the five vowels by:

pointing at random to a chart of vowels,
jumping on, or running to a letter games,
sorting games,
writing letters to dictation,
identifying vowels at the beginning of the names of the objects on opposite page,
listening to initial and middle vowels,
matching vowels and pictures,
anything else that may have proved popular so far.

Look at the alphabet chart again. Pick out the vowels.

THE CONSONANTS and FURTHER PROPORTION

Have the alphabet chart available so that the child can find and compare the letters indicated.

The rest of the letters in the alphabet are called consonants and you will find their sounds easy to learn.

Go through the alphabet identifying each letter as either a vowel or a consonant. The consonants are all easy to write if you remember that all letters are made up of circles or parts of circles and straight lines, and that they are all either tall or small.

All the ones we can write so far (the vowels) are small.
Point to others that are small—c, s, n, m, w, r, v, x, z.

Tall letters are twice as big—l, h, k, b, d. Put two small line templates one above the other to show 'tall', then two 'o's. Compare them with l and h templates and let children handle them. Do not use the sounds of these letters, just compare sizes.

Some 'smalls' have tails, and these tails go below the line, just like monkeys' tails, when the monkeys are sitting on a branch . . . j, q, y, p, g.

Compare these letters by drawing examples and handling templates.

Go through the alphabet getting children to identify each letter as tall or small, or small with a tail.

This is a very important step as it establishes proportion and can prevent much possible future confusion over the position of letters in relation to each other and to the line they are standing on.

Proportion

In the pronunciation of the sounds of consonants, great care must be taken to keep the consonants as clear as possible of a following vowel sound, e.g. 'b' may not be 'ba' or 'bu' but as nearly as possible just 'b'. Similarly 't', otherwise 'b' 'a' 't' will sound more like 'barter' than 'bat'. N.B. 'l' not 'la'; 'm' not 'mu'; 'n' not 'nu'. Get the lips and tongue in the correct position and just breathe the sound.

SIGHT WORDS

There is more than one way of finding out what a word says.

If we come to a word we do not know, we may either:

1. **work it out by the sounds of the letters;**
2. **recognize the whole shape of the word; or**
3. **make a reasonable guess, getting hints from other words and pictures.**

'the' is a word we often find and which we can get to know by looking at it so that we shall recognize it when we see it again.

Make up some sentences using 'the' (spoken only).

Write 'the' large, small and in various colours.

Homework: Cut out and paste on to a page all the 'the's you can find.

Some of the 'the's found will have capital letters, so mention, but do not yet elaborate on, the fact that letters have two forms, the lower case and the upper case or capital. If the term 'lower case' is used, then confusion between 'small' meaning size and 'small' meaning lower case will be avoided. Similarly, use 'capital' not 'big'. Keep 'small', 'tall', 'large' and 'big' to refer to the size of the letter, and 'lower case' and 'capital' to refer to the form or shape the letter takes.

Here is another word to find and cut out . . . and.

We shall call words we get to know by looking at them whole 'sight words'. 'the' and 'and' are our first sight words.

Make flash cards of 'the' and 'and'. The size of the flash cards may depend on whether there is a group, or just one child. This one, 10 cm × 5 cm, is suitable for group use:

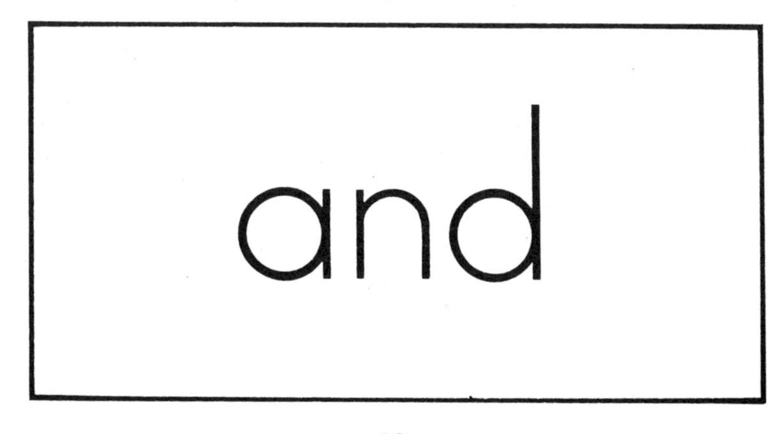

Try to keep the size and form of the letters consistent and based on the circles and straight lines being taught. Make duplicate copies and as more words are added they can be used, amongst other things, for the game of 'Snap'.

Another simple game even at this stage is to make several cards of each word and expose them quickly in succession on the table. If the child recognizes the word quickly, the card is his, and if not it goes to the dealer. Get faster and faster.
Examples of sight word flash cards are printed on p. 141. Paste the page on cardboard and cut out the words as needed.

POINTING ROUTINES

It is helpful from now on to establish a routine of pointing carefully and accurately to each letter. Explain that at the moment it is important and everyone must do it, but that later on when reading is quick, it will no longer be necessary.

The place and order of letters and words needs constant reinforcement and this is best done by pointing, not vaguely, but *very precisely*. It establishes ideas of position and one-to-one relationship, and gives practice with rhythm, number concepts and counting.

Pointing also helps children to learn to follow instructions accurately, which is of lasting and inestimable value.

Pointing may also be used to illustrate and establish spatial concepts such as top, next, bottom, left, right and the ordinal numeration first, second, third, etc.

Give plenty of practice in pointing to:

the first letter
the middle letter
the last letter
the top of the page
the bottom of the page
the first word
the last word, and so on.

Class or group lessons are made much easier when all the children can recognize these terms and follow them accurately and quickly.

abcdefghijklmnopqrstuvwxyz

Here is the first consonant we shall learn.

Find it on the alphabet chart.

'c' is the sound at the beginning of cat, cup, candle, coat, cabbage, carrot, cake, crumbs, cushion, collar.

Look at the pictures and say their names.

You can hear it at the end of these words:
luck, rack, sack, duck

and in the middle of these:
buckle, hiccoughs, second, secure.

Say the sound—'c'.

Whose name begins with this sound?

What are other names beginning with 'c' . . . Christopher, Catherine.

When introducing a new letter go through all the drills suggested for 'a'—writing in the air, writing on the desk, tracing templates, tracing in sand, feeling sandpaper letters, handling wooden templates, walking round a big letter drawn on the ground, or any other exercise that has proved helpful.

'c' is made by starting a circle at the same place at which we start an 'o', but we stop before joining up the circle.

Allow the child to compare and handle templates of 'o' and 'c'.

Write rows of 'c'.

Now write 'c' with 'a' and get the combined sound 'ca'
'c' with 'o' and get the combined sound 'co'
'c' with 'u' and get the combined sound 'cu'

Let the children write and read ca, co, cu. Call for suggestions of words starting with these sounds but do not write any further letters yet. The children will suggest all kinds of words—accept them but keep the emphasis on the sound of 'c'.

ca

co

cu

abcdefghijklmnopqrstuvwxyz

Find this letter on the alphabet chart.

't' is the sound at the beginning of
top, truck, toes, tap, ten, tiger, table, telephone, tulip.

(Take examples from the children.)

Say the sound—'t'.

Look at the pictures and say their names.

Hear it too in the middle of
little, fitted, patted.

The 't' sound is at the end of
cot, nut, net, sat.

These names begin with 't': Tommy, Terry, Timothy.
Can you think of some others?

't' is made by a tall straight line being crossed by a small line at exactly the height of a small letter. Although it is a 'tall' letter, it looks best if it is not too tall.

Draw 'o' to get proportion. Now draw a tall line and cross it with a short line at the height of the 'o'.

Follow usual preliminary drills.

Sound the 'ot' you have just written.

What does that say?

What if we put a 'c' in front of it?

Point firmly to each letter and sound each letter clearly.

Now we can write and read this word. Do it many times.

We can also write at **and** cat.

After preliminary practice of circles and straight lines of various kinds, practise writing all the letters so far known:

a o e i u c t

What words can we make from these letters?

cut cat tot at it

Note: deal only with those words whose sounds are consistent with the single simple sound so far taught for each letter, not, for example, 'coat' or 'out'.

Revise 'the': the cat
the cot

Revise 'and': the cat and the cot

Add all known words to flash cards.

Revise proportion, using all the letters in the alphabet, for 'tall', 'small' and 'small with a tail'.

abcdefghijklmnopqrstuvwxyz

'p' is a very useful 'small with a tail'.

Find it on the alphabet chart.

This letter has the sound 'p' as you hear it at the beginning of pot, picture, place, plant, people, paint, page, pear, puppy, pig, pond, pie, pastry, pan, poplars.

Look at the pictures and say their names.

Say the sound—'p'.

It is in the middle of happy, floppy, snapped.

Listen to it at the end of hop, clap, flap, bump.

Here are some names: Pat, Paul, Penny.

Here is a sentence with lots of 'p's:
Peter Piper picked a peck of pickled pepper.

Demonstrate with template lower case 'o' and tall line.

Place the line on top of the 'o' at left-hand side to show again how letters are made of circles and straight lines. Place template 'p' on top to show the exact correlation. Practise other popular drills.

We do the small line and tail first, starting at the right size for a 'small' and going below the line, but not too far. A good proportion for all descenders (tails) is half the length of an o beneath the line, but this may be too difficult for small children to grasp at first.

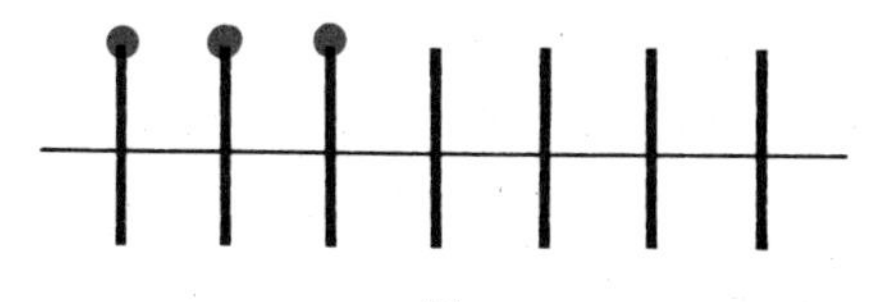

Do a line of these first.

Now we come up this line and near the top branch off to make a circle.

When you write it, say what you are doing to a rhythm—'down-up-round'.

Now we can make many more words to write and read:

up pup pop pip
pot pat pet pit
top tap tip
cop cap cup.

Blending sounds can be a little difficult for some children, so make the simple cardboard stand and letters as described on pp. 135–6. Place cards with 'c', 't', and 'p' on top of each other at the left, all the vowels in the middle, and 'p' and 't' at the end. Quick interchanges within each set make good fun and excellent practice for blending the sounds.

MORE SIGHT WORDS

Refer to page 39 for discussion of 'sight' words.

Revise 'the' and 'and'.

Here are more words we can get to know just by looking at them:

to **come** **I**

Add to your flash cards all words known so far and see that 'the', 'and', 'to', 'come' and 'I' are known. Also 'at', 'it', 'up'. Put flash cards in the long cardboard stand as described on page 135 and make sentences to be read out loud.
For example:

I come to the cat.

Check 'talls' and 'smalls' and then ask the child to copy the sentences into his writing book. Letters whose construction has been learnt must be of correct construction and proportion but be lenient with shapes of letters not yet taught, 'h' and 'm'.

abcdefghijklmnopqrstuvwxyz

S

Now we come to a letter which is fun to say and tricky to write.

Find it on the alphabet chart.

The sound is 's' as you hear it at the beginning of snake, sock, sausage, soap, sail, school, sun, swing, saw, sticks, squirrel, spider, snowdrops.

Look at the pictures and say their names.

Say the sound 's'.

It is in the middle of hissed, mist, fast, lesson, blossom.

It is at the end of lots, hats, pots, curious, famous.

These names begin with 's': Sara, Sandra, Sam.

Sometimes 's' has a hard sound, as in 'as' and 'is'. We put 'a' in front of 's' and have 'as'. We put 'i' in front of 's' and have 'is'. Write these two sight words on paper or blackboard, and add 'was'.

Now we have another useful word, a funny one—'was'. 'Was' looks as though it should say was (with 'a' as in cat) but it is peculiar and says was (wos). So just learn it.

Write it in the air.

Look at it on the board, then close your eyes and see it.

Add 'as', 'is' and 'was' to flash cards.

's' is based on the shape and size of 'o'. Find template 'o' and fit 's' on to it. You start to write it by starting in the same place as you do for the 'o', then draw across the circle and go backwards round the bottom.

Start off by making circles, then fit 's' inside them in a different colour.

Make use of preliminary drills.

Write a line of 's'.

Revise some known words and make them into a list such as:

cat
pot
sit
cup
tap

What happens when we add 's' to the ends of these words?

Write two columns of words, the first like the one above and the second with 's' added.

Notice that now there is more than one middle letter.

Point to the first letter and say it; point to the middle letters and say them; point to the last letter and say it.

Take examples of words with lots of middle letters:
chimpanzee, pancakes, buffalo

Draw a cat and under it write—the cat sits up

Now we can make many more words and more interesting sentences.

Get children to make sentences from:
the, and, at, it, up, to, come, I, is, was
with known readable sound words. At first write the sentences clearly on the blackboard or paper asking the children to dictate the letters to you. Make mistakes with spelling and letter proportions and let them

correct you. Let the children copy the correct sentences. Do not let any mistakes pass. Finally, let them construct their own sentences, writing and reading as they go. Put good examples up on the wall either at home or in the schoolroom where they can be read and enjoyed.

LETTER, WORD AND SENTENCE

It is here useful to make sure that the terms *letter*, *word* and *sentence* are quite clearly understood and differentiated.

Letters stand for sounds.
Call out sounds of letters for the children to write down. Check to see they are correct.

Words are groups of letters.
Call out words already learned where the construction of the letters is known. Ask for them to be written down, telling the child to listen carefully to thc sounds of the letters, and check to see that they are right.

Sometimes 'a' is a letter and has the 'a' sound we know, as in the words hat, map, cat.

But sometimes it stands by itself and is a word. Then it has the sound 'u', as in

a cup
a tap
a pot

Draw pictures of these things and write the words beneath them.

Read: **a cup**
the cup
a top
the top
a pet
the pet
a pit
the pits
the pots
the caps

Revise flash cards and make new ones as necessary.

Sentences are groups of words.
It is obvious that sentences made from the limited vocabulary so far available will be stilted and in some cases a little odd. The situation rapidly improves as further consonants are mastered. The important point is that all the words used are completely within the control and understanding of the learner from the point of view of writing and reading. Let the children read the following sentences aloud (they may

need to be written on a blackboard) and then get them to write them out. They should copy accurately from the examples at first, paying careful attention to the proportions of the letters.

I come to the top
a pot is up at the top
a cat comes to the cup
pat the cat
tip a pot up
tap the cups
sip the cup

Now get them to write the sentences out when they are dictated. The use of initial capital letters and full stops is dealt with later.

abcdefghijklmnopqrstuvwxyz

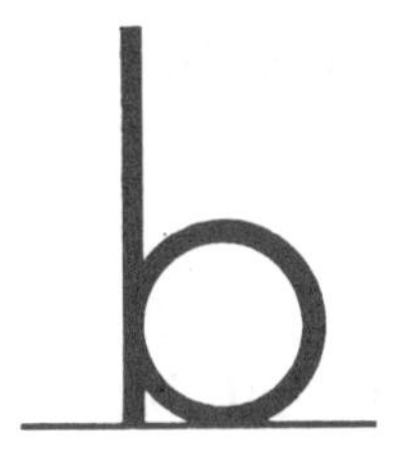

Find this letter on the alphabet chart.

'b' is the sound at the beginning of:
bus, bicycle, balloon, bed, ball, book, bowl, baby, banana.

Look at the pictures—say their names.

Say the sound—'b'.

Think of some words beginning with 'b'.

It is in the middle of trouble, able, bubble, wobble, nibble and at the end of sob, cab, scrub.

'b' begins these names: Bob, Barbara, Bill.
Where else is it?

It makes a *bursting* kind of sound and it is a *bulge*.

Chant: 'b begins big and bursts out the back'

Draw:

Take the template of the tall line and place it on top of the left side of the template 'o'. Take template 'b' and place it on top to prove the shape.

To write 'b' start with a tall line, go up to the height of a small letter and branch off to make a circle.

Make sure your circle is just the same as an 'o'.

Remember: 'b' begins big and bursts out the back.

Use preliminary drills as necessary.

Practise lines of 'b'.

Read, write and read again:

bus bat bits cub tab

it is cut and I sob

cut it up

the bus and the cab come up

the cat bit it

I bet the bat is at the top

Here is another word to learn by sight: 'see'.

The two 'e's together say 'ee'.

Write and read: see

see it is cut up

I see the cat in the bus

see the bits of the cup

abcdefghijklmnopqrstuvwxyz

A letter made of a circle and a straight line with a tail is ‘g’.

Find it on the alphabet chart.

The sound is ‘g’ which you hear at the beginning of good, girl, goose, giggle, gold, gate, green, goat, grass, grain.

Look at the pictures and say their names.

Say the sound—‘g’.

It is in the middle of begin, forget, gurgle, and at the end of peg, mug, fog, drag, dig.

Names beginning with ‘g’ are Gertrude, Grandma.

Demonstrate with the template ‘o’. First add the small straight line, giving a.

The tail of ‘g’ is a straight line with part of a circle at the bottom. Put a g on top showing relationship of these shapes to each other.

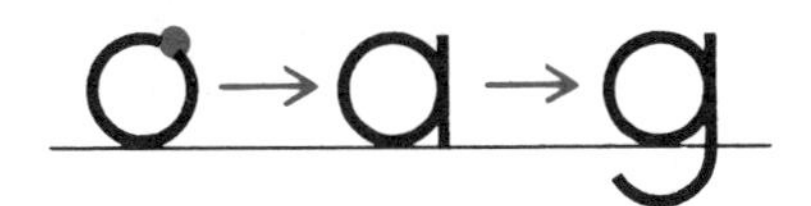

Make sure the ‘o’ is started in the correct place.

Do not make the tail too long (see note on descenders under ‘p’, page 51)

Go through usual preliminary drills.

Say a rhythm while writing—‘*round* and *up* and *down* with a tail’.

Write a line of g.

Write and read:

got get big bug gap pegs
come and see the big bug in the bag

Draw a bug in a bag and put labels on it like this:

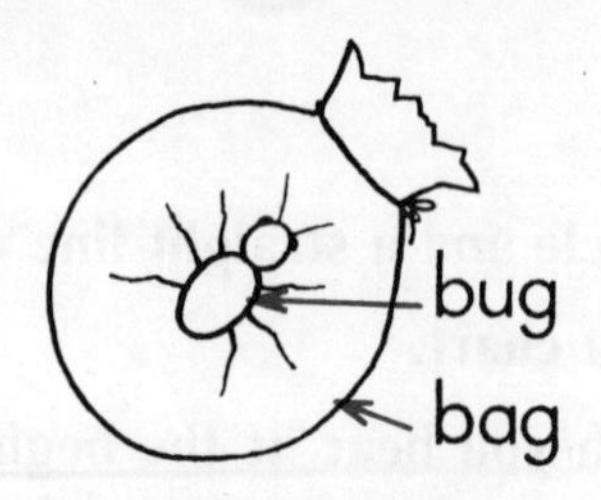

the bug got in the bag
the bug in the bag was big
see the pig in a gap

Draw a pig in a gap and label it.

See if you can draw what you read here:

the pig tugs at the bag and it pops

REVISION

See what words we can make from these letters.
See that only the simple sounds so far taught are used.

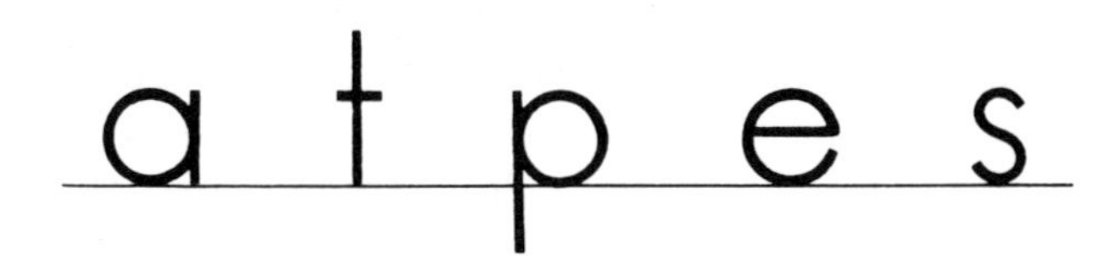

Now see what words you can make by yourself from these letters:

Revise vowel sounds, writing and reading:

a e i o u

Put one of these vowels between these two letters to make a word:

r g

Now a different vowel:

r g

Now a different vowel:

r g

Put different vowels between these letters to make as many words as you can:

c p p g b g
s t p p t p

Can you make more words by putting 's' on the end?

Draw and label:

a tap
a cup
eggs
a dog
a pot
bags

THE USE OF A PERSONAL DICTIONARY

SEQUENCE IN THE ALPHABET

At this point the child could be given a notebook in which to enter all the words he knows. An indexed notebook can be used, or a notebook can be prepared by the teacher or parent with one letter printed clearly at the top of each page. Alternatively, use the companion dictionary to this book: *My First Reading and Writing Dictionary.*

The use of the personal dictionary will give a sense of the other letters to come and will begin to give an idea of the alphabetical sequence of letters.

This idea can be introduced by considering the alphabet line printed at the bottom of any of the illustrated letter pages and asking 'is "a", "p", "c" etc. near the beginning of the alphabet, or in the middle, or near the end?'

To begin using the dictionary, help the pupil to write in words he knows. Let him say the word, listen to the sound it starts with, find the letter on the alphabet line and then find the page. When the word starts with an unusual sound that has not yet been met explain that it *is* a tricky one and has a special sound. Show the child which page to write it on.

When the pupil asks for the spelling of a word for his dictionary get him into the habit of bringing it to you open at the right page. This is good practice for him and time-saving in the classroom.
Encourage an interesting and adventurous collection of words from reading-books and experiences so that written work quickly expresses what a child really wants to write down.

For extra reading practice, when adding a new word let the pupil read all the words written so far on that page.

Get children to read each other's lists for a particular letter. Let children work in pairs, reading aloud the words from their lists for letters chosen at random.

abcdefghijklmnopqrstuvwxyz

Find this letter on the alphabet chart.

The tall straight line itself has a sound. It is ‘l’, the sound at the beginning of lemon, lovely, lake, lamp, light, letter, lion, leaves.

Look at the pictures and say their names.

Say the sound—‘l’.

Hear it in the middle of hilly, pulled, fellow, pillow, yellow, believe, police.

And at the end of apple, simple, fill, spell, school.

You know how to make it—straight, and twice the height of the ‘o’.

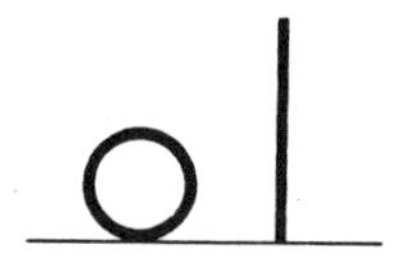

Go through the usual practices which children will delight in with so easy a letter.

Write and read: lot lap let leg.

Often there are two ‘l’s together but although we write two ‘l’s, the sound is just the same as one ‘l’:
bell sell bill pill tell till.

Keep the proportions of the letters correct.

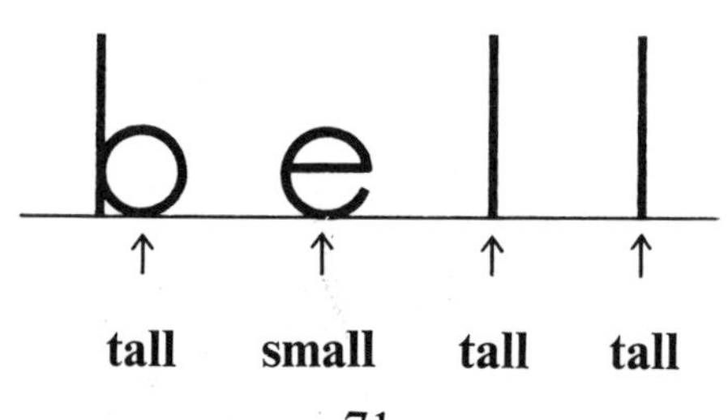

Read, write and read again:

tug the bell till it is up

sell the lot to us

tell the cub to get it

let the cats tug it to bits

sell the logs in bags

come and see the pup get a pill

Sometimes there are two 's's written together, but here again the sound is the same as just one 's'. Sound these words with just one 's':

less toss

Write and read:

I had less to see

see the cub toss it up

Revise flash cards of
to, come, I, at, it, up, the, and,
is, was, see and other favourites.

Read, pointing to each letter and sounding it, and then reading the whole word: 'l', 'o', 't': lot

lot	**let**	**lit**
got	**get**	**gap**
pig	**peg**	**pop**
sit	**set**	**sat**
sell	**sill**	**pill**

Now write these words and then read them again.

Here is another sight word: <u>will</u>
Read it in these sentences:

I will get up

will the pup sit up

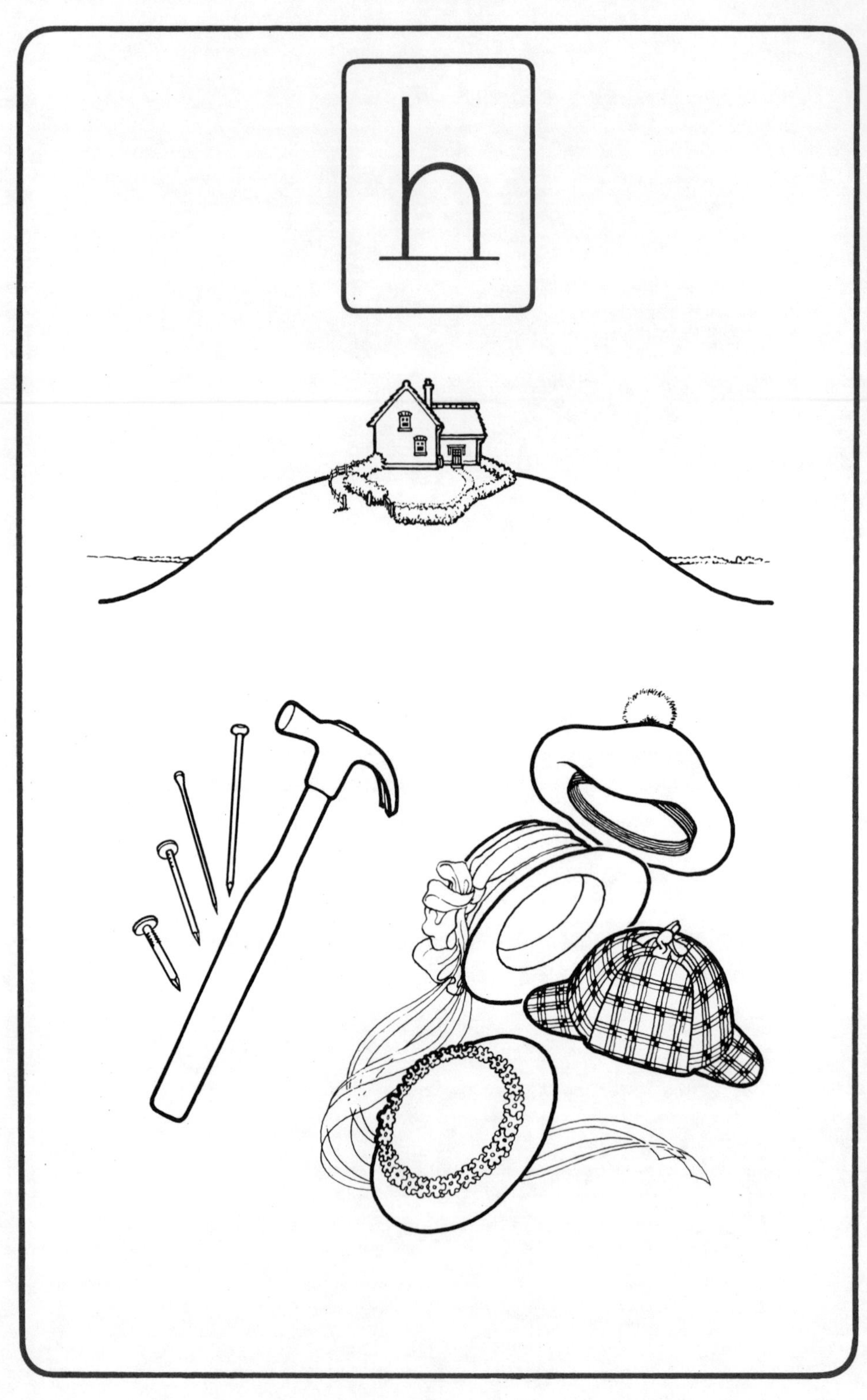

abcdefghijklmnopqrstuvwxyz

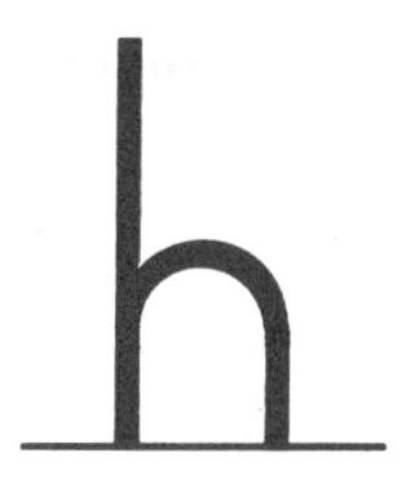

Now we come to a family of letters made of straight lines with a curve (part of a circle) across the top.

They are:

Take template 'h' and fit template 'n' on top to show the relationship. Identify tall and small letters. Fit 'l' on to 'n' and make 'h'. Give children letters to compare and fit on to each other.

First we shall learn 'h'.

Find it on the alphabet chart.

The sound is 'h' as you hear it at the beginning of house, hill, heavy, hello, hot, hammer, hand, honey, hat, hedge.

Look at the pictures and say their names.

Say the sound—'h'.

It is in the middle of perhaps, behave, behind.

Here are some names: Harry, Henry, Helen.

To make 'h' start with a tall line, starting at the top, and come back half way up (to the size of a small letter) and make a curve out of the side as round the top of a circle, and then come straight down to the line.

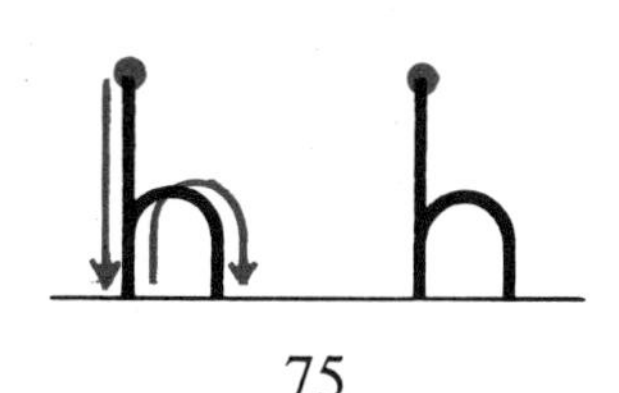

Not too fat (demonstrate), **not too thin** (demonstrate):

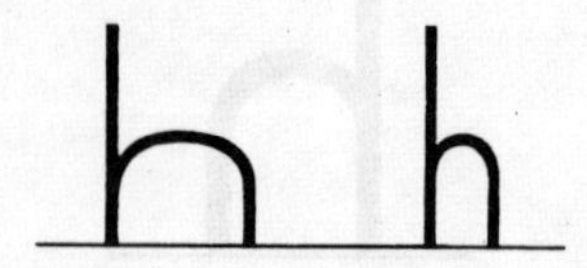

Go through the usual drills.

Write a line of 'h', chanting 'down, up, round, down'.

Write these words:
hut hat hit hot hop

Write and read these sentences:

the hut was up the hill

it is a hot cup

his pup has got big legs

abcdefghijklmnopqrstuvwxyz

Find this letter on the alphabet chart.

It sounds at the beginning of:
nuts, nail, nibble, never, number, nine, neck, nest, necklace.

Look at the pictures and say their names.

It is in the middle of:
beginning, enough, and, panic,
bend, funny, running

You hear it at the end of:
hen, bun, open, fun, sun, in, on

'n' is a small letter, just like the bottom of the 'h'.

Show templates again. Follow helpful preliminary practices.

Write a line of 'n', saying: 'down, up, round, down'.

Write:

nut not nip hen

I can not get the hen to sit in the bin

I did not let the cat get in the net

come to the hut on the hill to see the pets

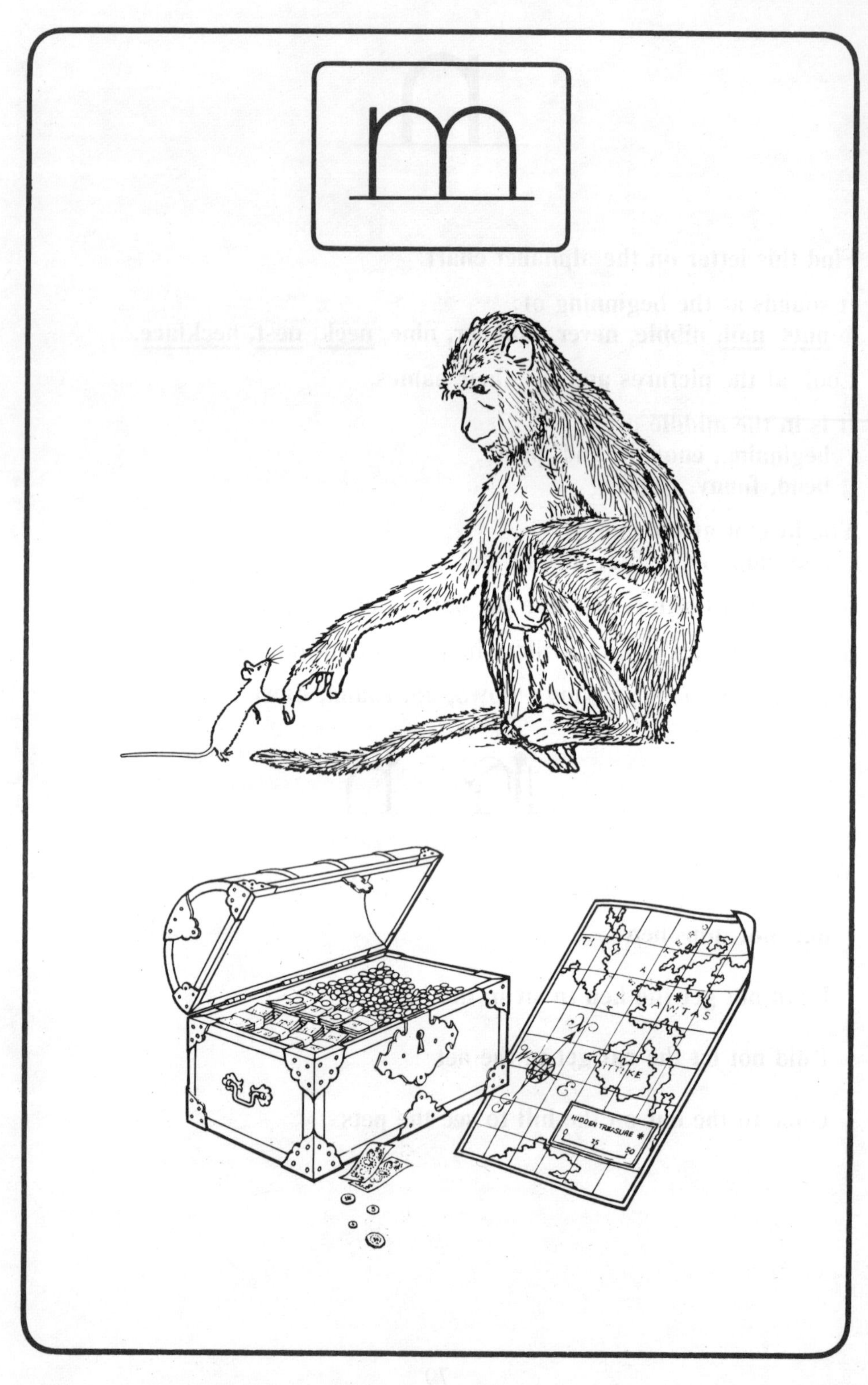

abcdefghijklmnopqrstuvwxyz

'm' is the sound at the beginning and in the middle of 'mummy'.

Say the sound—'m'.

Find it on the alphabet chart.

Hear it in mouse, man, most, milk, money, mug, matches, map, monkey.

Look at the pictures and say their names.

Hear it in these words: him, farmer, coming, blooming, alarm.

What are some names beginning with this sound?

Compare templates of 'n' and 'm'.

Write it like two 'n's—down, up round, down, up round, down.

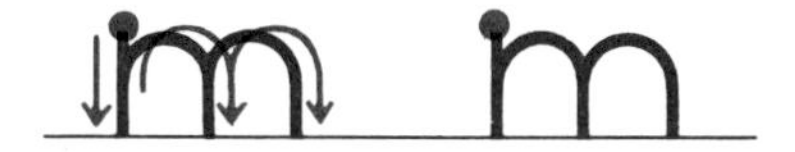

Follow useful practices.

Write a line of 'm'.

Write and read:

men mum mat mug
I met a man up at the mill
will the hens nip him
the men will get ham and eggs
come and get nuts in bags
it spilt on the mat
I can mop it up mum
pin the hem up
peg it on
the men at the pits get a bit hot
will the man sell the big pigs
the hens get in the bins
let him sell a lot of pegs

abcdefghijklmnopqrstuvwxyz

r

'r' is the sound at the beginning of 'rain'.

Say the sound— 'r'.

Find it on the alphabet chart.

Listen, and you will hear it at the beginning of red, raspberry, ruler, ribbon, rose, rabbit, river, rushes.

Look at the pictures and say their names.

Listen to 'r' in the middle of purring, surround, porridge, arise, parade.

Roger, Ray and Rosemary all begin with this sound.

It is easy to write as it is just like the beginning of the 'n', stopping after the curve on top.

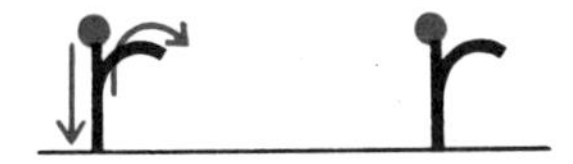

Show templates of 'r' fitting over 'n'.
Compare 'h', 'n', 'm', 'r' templates.

Make it not too fat, not too thin, and the same size as all the other 'smalls'.

Do not forget the usual drills for new letters.

Write a line of 'r'.

Write and read:

run rat rig rob

a cat can rip up rugs

run and get the mop

the man he met sells rams and pigs

Help children find three-letter words they can sound from these letters:

o a b m r g s p

Fill in the gaps with vowels:

h t	**h m**	**r g**
h t	**h m**	**r g**
b t	**m t**	**p p**
b t	**m t**	**p p**
h s	**r n**	**s t**
h s	**r n**	**s t**
c p	**t g**	**b n**
c p	**t g**	**b n**

NAMES OF LETTERS

All letters have names as well as sounds.

Sometimes a letter will say its name instead of its sound.

The sound of the letter 'e', as we already know, is 'e' as in egg. This is a short sound.

Its name is 'ee', which is a long sound. It has this sound in me.

Sound it: 'm' 'ee'—me.

In a syllable or short word where there is no consonant following the vowel, the sound is long.

These words also sound 'ee', not 'e':
he be

Here is a new sight word: she

Read these sentences:
see me
he can see me
she can come to me
can he be in the hut
be still

Sometimes 'o' says its name—'oh', as in 'no' and 'go'.
This is its long sound.

Read these sentences three times:
let us go and pop on the hats
I can see no hats
go to his bag and get me a big ham
she will not let me
I see he has got me a bell
let us go up the hill and get nuts to sell in bags

Add no, go, he, she, be, me to flash cards.

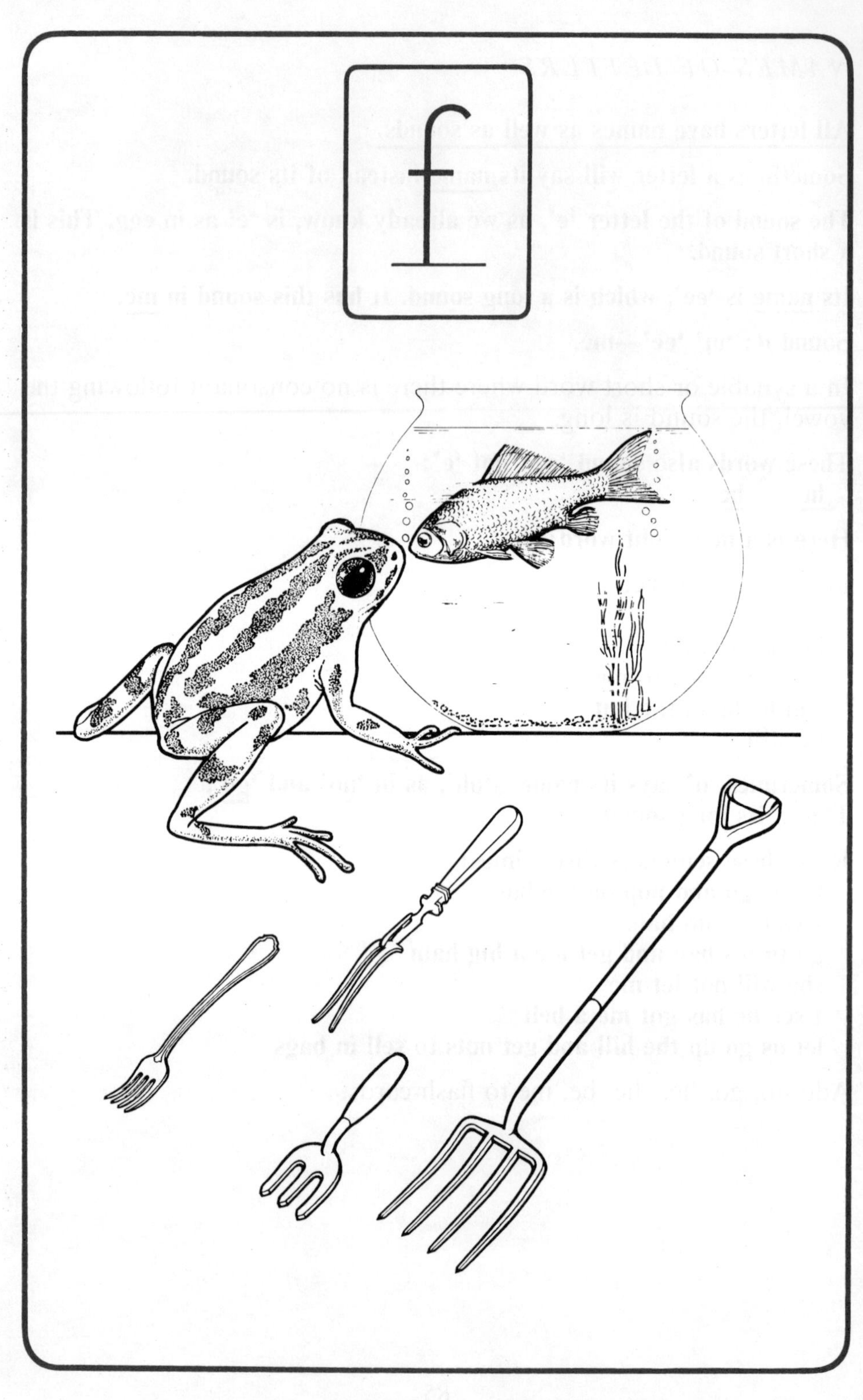

abcdefghijklmnopqrstuvwxyz

Find this letter on the alphabet chart.

Another curve and straight line letter is 'f'. It is a tall letter which you can hear at the beginning of:
funny, feather, fast, fish, father,
face, frog, football, fork.

Look at the pictures and say their names.

Say the sound—'f'.

It is in the middle of:
buffalo, muffled, baffle, different,
soft, refill.

And at the end of:
scarf, sniff, scoff.

The name of 'f' is 'eff'.

To write it we start at the same place in which we start an 'o' but at the height of a tall letter. Curve round and then come straight down, and put a neat little cross just at the height of a small letter, as you did with the 't'.

Follow the usual practices.

Write a line of 'f'.

When we sound a word with two 'f's together we sound 'f' only once.

Sound out—off cuff puff

Read these sentences:
I got off the bus
the cat got off the rug
his cuff is off

Write and read:

fun if fill fat muff

'of' is a useful word, but notice the 'f' has a hard sound, not soft as in 'off'.

Write and read:

the pup is a lot of fun

the fat pig can get up to the top of the hill

if she has had ten buns she must stop

can he get the top off the tin

I can hop off the top of the steps

'for' is a word to learn.

run for the bus

get it for me

come up for fun

cats go for rats

Make sure you know the difference between 'of' and 'for'. So that you do not make a mistake, make sure that you

GET THE SOUND OF THE FIRST LETTER

N.B. This is a most important rule. Chant it many times. It helps to preclude the habit of making reversals (spelling and reading backwards).

The game described on p. 40 using three cards each of 'of' and 'for' will quickly fix these words in memory and give practice of the important rule above.

Read and write:

the top of the cup

come for the bat

a bag of nuts

sit up for me

a lot of figs

Here are two more sight words:

from **have**

Add to flash cards: of, for, off, from, have, if, but.

Make sentences from these words (the words could be printed on cards and then re-arranged):

1. **I bell see the can**
2. **fell his off hat**
3. **bun I have a can**
4. **him let me see**
5. **the tip up bin**
6. **sell the us hut let**
7. **I run can up bed to**
8. **hen eggs the has**
9. **not he is sad**
10. **tell I him can**

abcdefghijklmnopqrstuvwxyz

Another letter in the 'circle and straight line' family is 'd'.

Find it on the alphabet chart.

Hear it at the beginning of:
duck, dig, daisy, dance, doll, dish, delightful, dog, door, drawer, daffodil.

Look at the pictures and say their names.

Say the sound—'d'.

Say and listen: I did a dashing dance. Where did the 'd' sounds come in that sentence?

It is in the middle of:
middle

And at the end of:
end

Hear it in the middle of:
puddle, fiddle, muddle, pedal.

It is at the end of: pod, lead, fade, mud.

The name of 'd' is 'dee'.

Show template 'o' and place the tall straight line on top of the right-hand side to construct 'd'. Place template 'd' on top to fit.

We write 'd' simply by making the 'o', *starting at the right place*, but when we have joined it up, we keep on going up to make a tall straight line and then come down the same line until we meet the line it is standing on.

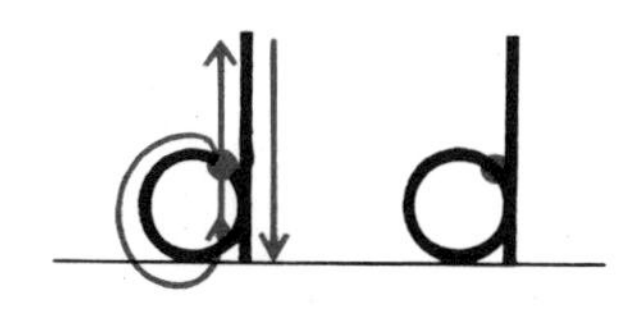

Follow the usual practices.

Write a line of 'd'.

Write and read:

dad did

did dad dig it up

it had red dots on it

did the hens nip off the buds

the dog drags his bed

dad is still in bed

DISTINGUISHING BETWEEN 'd' AND 'b'

If confusion has arisen between these two letters, take a special lesson to clear it.

Take a large piece of paper and make a chart with the children watching and contributing.
Divide the paper down the middle.
Make a large, coloured 'd' to head the 'd' side and a similar 'b' on the 'b' side.
Ask the children to describe where 'd' starts. Get them to chant '"d" goes round, then up and *d*own.'
Ask them 'Where does "b" start?'
Chant: ' "b" begins big and bursts out behind'.
Draw further 'd' and 'b' with constructional arrows and the two chants underneath.
Get the children to suggest words beginning with 'd' and write them in the 'd' column. Similarly with 'b'.
Read altogether over the columns several times.
Repeat at daily intervals or as necessary.

The wall chart could look like this:

So far all the letters taught have been 'lower case' letters. If this term is regularly used, the children will understand it readily. The term 'capital' is convenient to use for upper case letters. Avoid the use of 'big' and 'little' to describe upper and lower case letters, as this becomes confusing when proportion is discussed. Keep to 'tall' and 'small' for describing relative size.

All of the letters we have learned to read and write so far may be written as capital letters also, but they still have the same sound.

a may be written as a capital A.

b may be written as a capital B.

Sometimes the capital has the same shape as the lower case letter, such as c, C and s, S; sometimes it is similar, such as t, T and b, B; and sometimes it is quite different: g, G.

Capital letters are always 'tall'. Where a midpoint is needed for form it is usually at half height, at the height of a 'small' letter:

oABEFGHKPRXY

Go through all the letters so far learned.

Make a large chart while children are watching, showing the capitals of known small letters.

We use capital letters at the beginnings of sentences, such as:
Let us go
Fill it up

and for beginnings of names of people:
Ann, Peter

and places:
London, Amsterdam

and names of days and months and special occasions:
Monday, June, Christmas.

Let the children supply many examples of each of these.

Ordinary words do not need capital letters at the beginning.

Don't forget: the sound of the capital letter is the same as the sound of the small letter.

Sometimes the whole word may be written in capital letters.

Sound these words out:
UP IN TO DOGS

Find all the capital T's you can in the newspaper and in magazines. Cut them out and paste them in your book. Do this with other capital letters also.

From now on, each day revise one known letter. Write a line of the small letter, then a line of its capital, and then capital and small letter together.

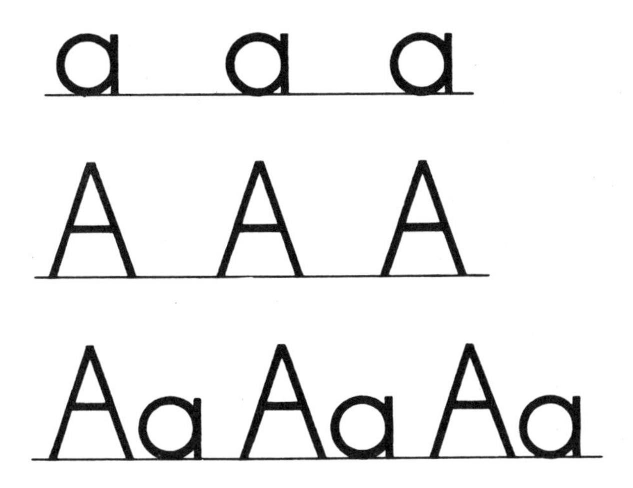

Constantly refer to and check proportion.

Then practise words containing the chosen letter:

at ant Ann

Never mix capital and lower case letters in one word (except for the capital letter at the beginning of the special words mentioned). Write out all these words, putting capital letters and lower case letters in the right places:
toM egG fRom heN BiLL bAt gEt
boB buS tIn toP haT Rug ann

FULL STOPS

Sentences start with a capital letter and end with a full stop.

A full stop is a dot put on the line after the last word in the sentence.

Find some full stops in books.

Write the sentences on page 59, making sure that the word at the beginning of the sentence starts with a capital letter and that there is a full stop at the end.

Chant 'sentences start with a capital letter and end with a full stop' many times, and often refer back to it.

Names must always be written with capital letters.

Write and read these names:

Ron	**Bill**	**Pam**
Ted	**Ann**	**Fred**
Dan	**Tom**	**Bob**
Pat		

Draw coloured arrows joining the lower case letters with their capital letters.

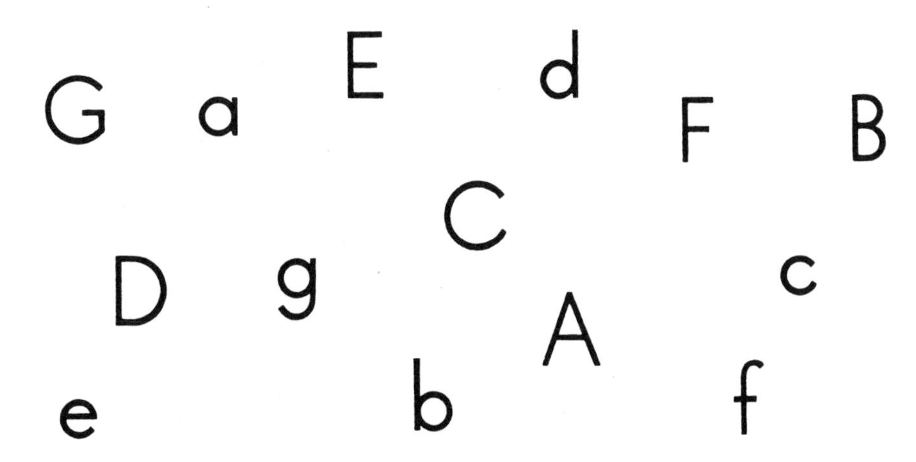

Write lower case letters beside these capital letters:

C	**E**	**S**	**A**	**O**
T	**B**	**P**	**H**	**M**

Write capital letters beside these lower case letters:

a	**n**	**s**	**c**	**u**
i	**f**	**h**	**e**	**p**

Write the capital and lower case for these letters (dictate all letters so far studied).

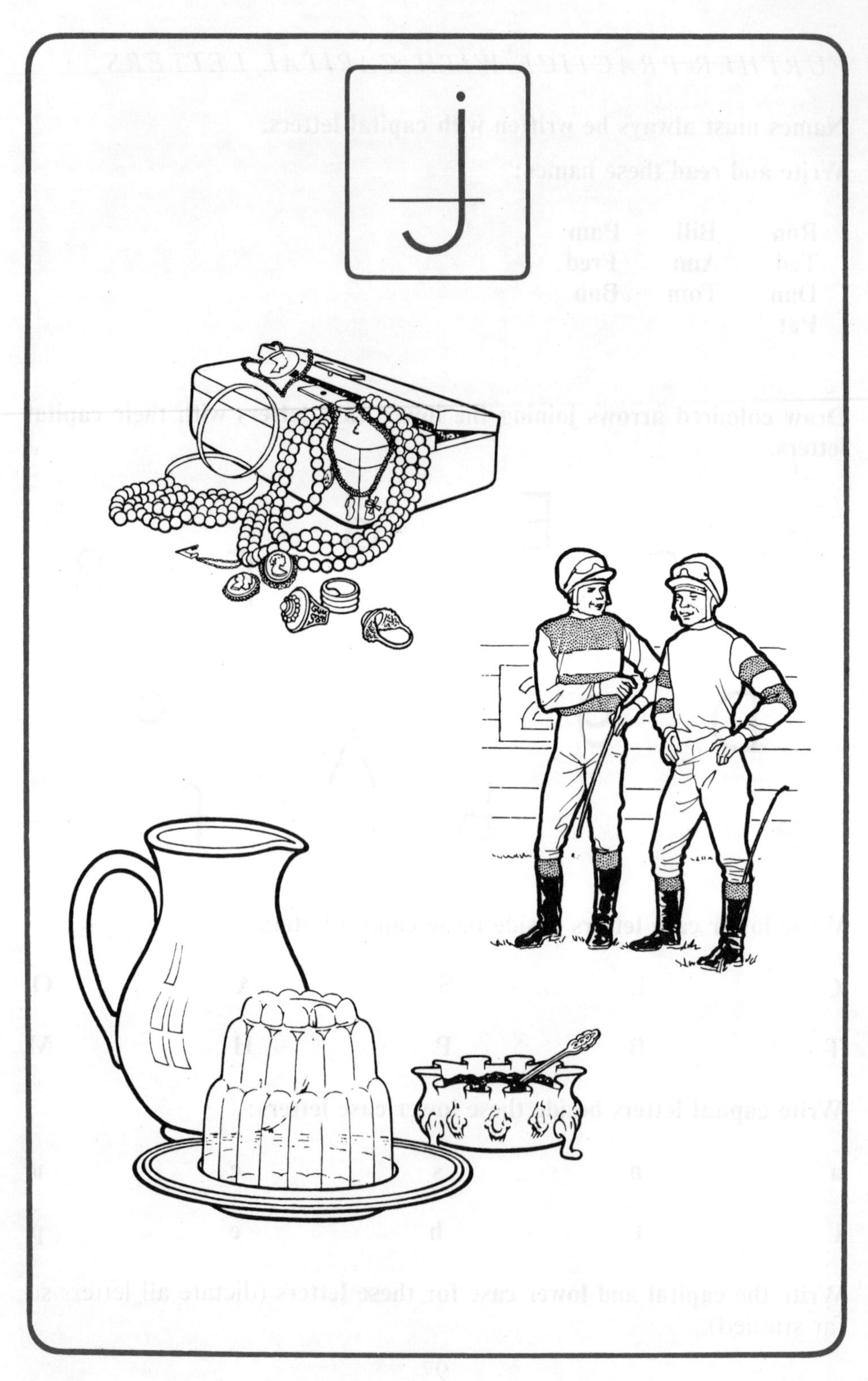

abcdefghijklmnopqrstuvwxyz

j is the sound at the beginning of:
jump.

Find it on the alphabet chart.

Listen for it at the beginning of:
jersey, Jim, Jill, jolly, jug, jewel, jelly, jam, jockey.

Look at the pictures and say their names.

Say the sound—'j'.

Listen for it in the middle of:
object, subject, reject, enjoy.

The name of 'j' is 'jay'.

Make a row of 'i'. Is 'i' small or tall?

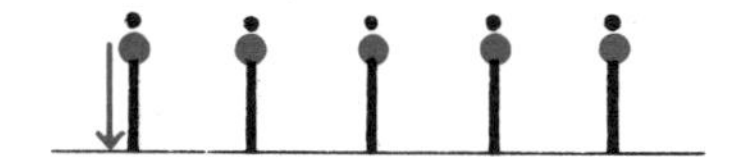

j is small with a tail. It is a small 'i' with a tail, like 'g', straight down and curved at the bottom.

Compare templates of i, j and g.

Write j by making the down line first and adding the dot afterwards.

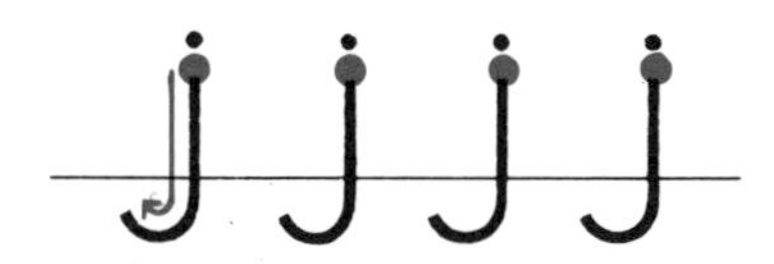

Capital J is like capital T, but has a curve at the bottom, sitting on the line.

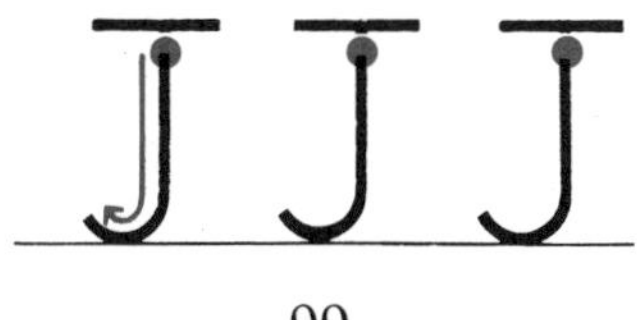

Add the little line at the top after the down line.
Make a line of capital J.
Now write a line of Jj:

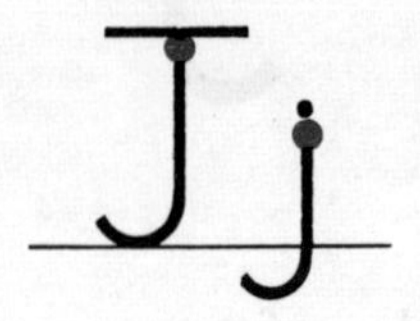

Write and read:

jam jet Jill Jim

Let us go and have jam Bill.

Jill had a job to fill the big red jug.

Jan can get the dogs to jump.

QUESTION MARKS

Have you remembered to start the sentences with a capital letter and end them with a full stop? If the sentence is a question, it ends with a question mark instead of a full stop. A question mark looks like this: ? Write a line of question marks.

Write and read:

Can Jan jump?

Will he come?

Can Jim get up the hill?

abcdefghijklmnopqrstuvwxyz

Find this letter on the alphabet chart.

As well as small 'c', there is a tall 'k'. It is often found with the small 'c' and together they just make one 'k' sound.

'k' is at the beginning and end of kick; sound it—

Listen: key, kettle, king, kitchen, kite.

Look at the pictures and say their names.

It is the sound in the middle of:
bucking, making, baking, rocking, waking.

It is the sound at the end of:
bleak, rake, woke, smoke.

The name of this 'k' is 'kay'.

The 'k' is similar to the 'h'. (Compare templates).

Instead of the hump of the 'h', a short line slants in, touches half way down and bounces back.

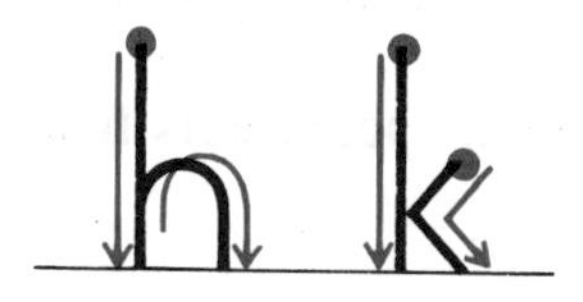

Make a line of good 'h's.

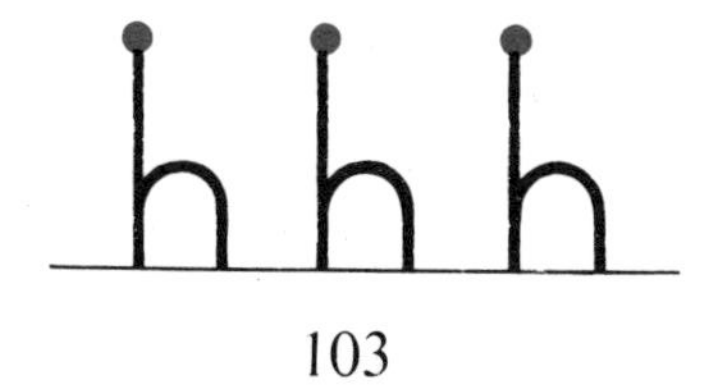

Now make another line, but like this:

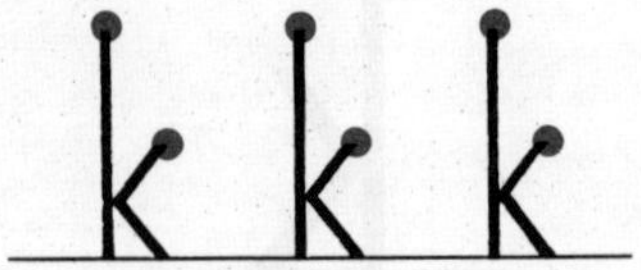

Capital ‘k’ looks very similar, but the sloping line starts from the tall position:

Now write a line of Kk:

Remember, ‘ck’ has the sound of just one ‘k’.

Write and read:

kick duck rack Mick milk pick

He can lick the jam pot.

Get a sack for the sick hen.

The clock ticks.

Get the big socks off.

Ducks peck, cats lick, pups suck.

COMMAS

The little mark like a full stop with a tail is called a 'comma'. We sometimes use it to show a little pause between words in a sentence. Here is another sentence with a comma:

Tom, the milk is here.

Where would you put commas in these sentences?

Come on we must run.

Tim get the hens in.

SYLLABLES

Up until now, all the words we have written and read have been of one part. Now we will look at words made up of two parts.

We call these parts syllables. To know the syllables of a word helps us to spell the word because syllables are always short, and even very long words can be divided up into short syllables which we can read and write.

Like this: um brel la   him self

Notice—every syllable has a vowel sound.

Try to divide these words into syllables (teacher write and read these words slowly):

suntan unplug dismiss
softly refill begin dustpan

Here are words of two syllables:

can not	**for get**
up on	**for got**
un til	**in to**

Try them in these sentences:

Bob will go on until the end.

I cannot tuck in the flaps.

Ann forgot to lick the stamp.

It was fun to run upon the sand.

Let us jump into the back, Dad.

Now write these sentences to dictation and read what you have written.

Add these two-syllable words to the flash cards.

USE OF CHARTS

Large clear charts demonstrating number, colour, and the days of the week are available from the publisher. They are based on designs printed at the end of this book. Hang them in prominent places around the room.

Go over these charts and see they are understood, but the spelling of the words is for reference, not yet to be learned by heart.

The children can now learn to construct sentences from sight words they know, sound words they can construct, and words seen on the reference charts. This gives practice in looking up words in different places. Unknown words can be written by the teacher in the child's individual dictionary note-book, getting the child to produce the book open at the right letter. For example:

I	see	five	purple	buds.
↑	↑	↑	↑	↑
sight word	sight word	from number chart	from colour chart	work out from sounds

Further examples are:

She has three green pills as she is sick.

He can get six white hens on Monday.

abcdefghijklmnopqrstuvwxyz

v

There is another family of letters made up of sloping lines, still straight, but sloping from top to bottom, either to the left or to the right.

Lets's try some sloping straight lines.

First left to right, always starting at the top:

Now from right to left, starting at the top:

Now first and then joined at the bottom.

We have made a 'v', the sound at the beginning of:

very, varnish, verse, view, van,
vase, violin, vacuum cleaner, violet.

You can hear the sound in the middle of:

ever never divide leaving evening every

Listen to it at the end of:

nerve brave cave believe

Look at the pictures and say their names.

Say the sound—'v'.

Where is it on the alphabet chart?

Write a line of 'v'.

Its capital is exactly the same, but twice the size:

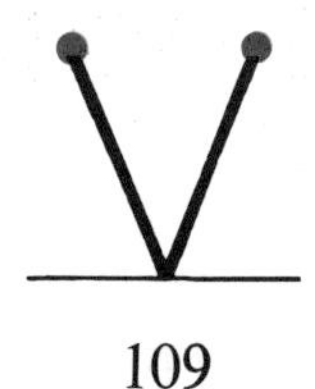

Try a line of both:

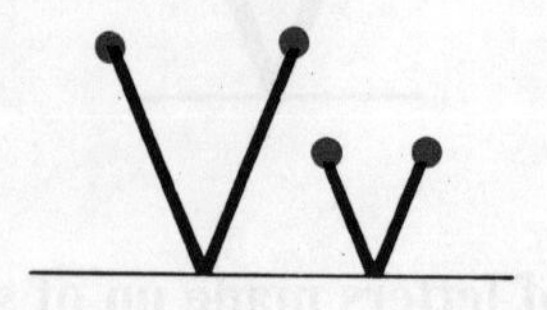

Its name is 'Vee'.

Write and read these words:

van vat vet

Is the van a red one?

The vet had ten green ducks.

(From colour chart).

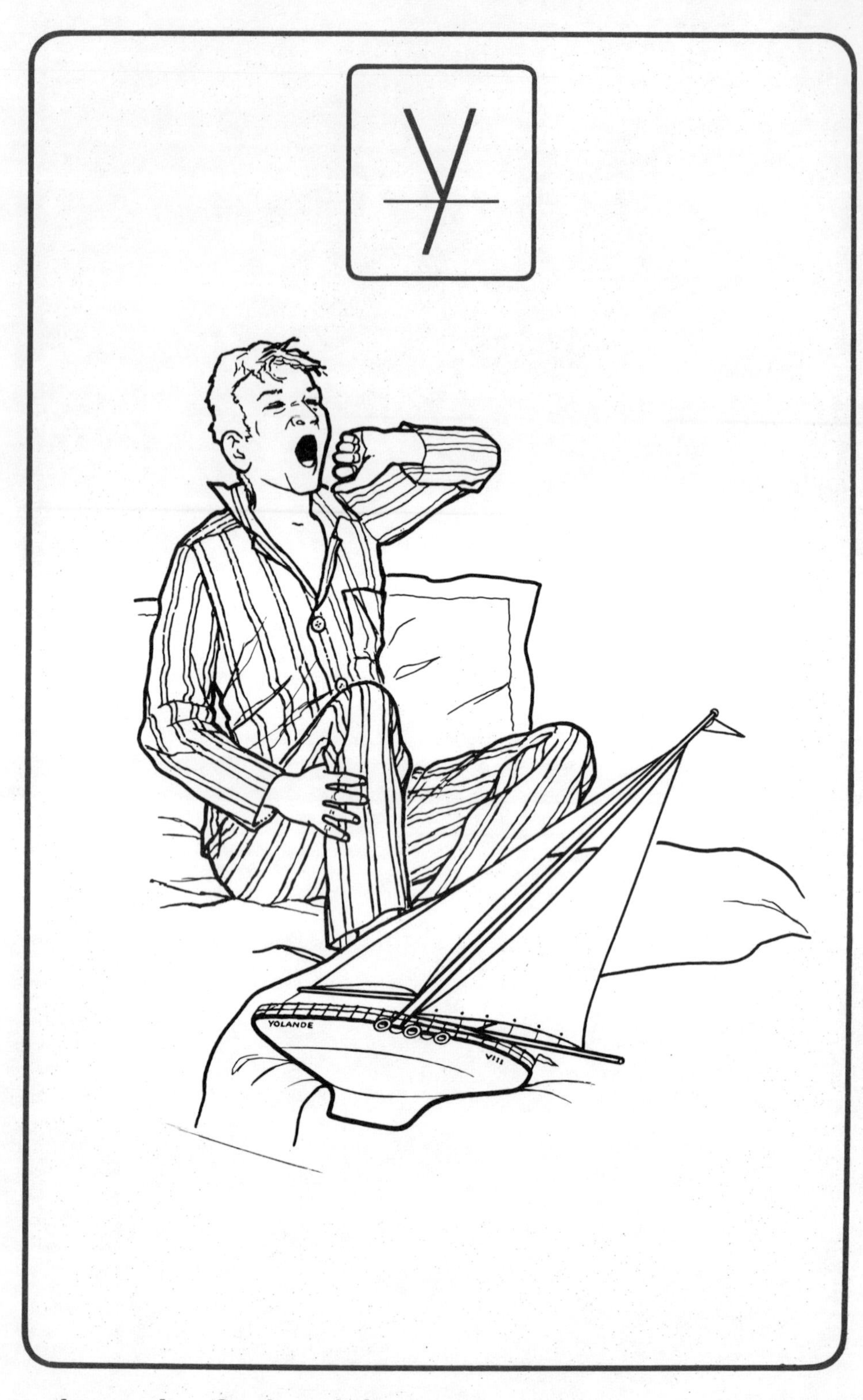

abcdefghijklmnopqrstuvwxyz

Find this letter on the alphabet chart.

'y' is the sound at the beginning of:
yellow, yesterday, you, yes, young,
year, <u>yawn,</u> <u>yacht.</u>

Look at the pictures and say their names.

Say the sound—'y'.

It is in the middle of:
beyond.

Its name is 'wy' (rhyming with 'try').

As a small letter it is made just like a 'v', but when the second line comes down, it continues on to form a tail beneath the line:

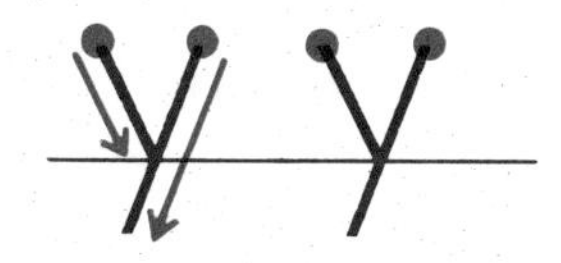

Write a line of 'y'.

Capital 'Y' is made by making a 'v', starting where we start tall letters:

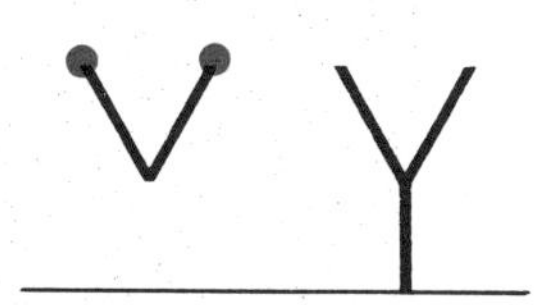

and adding a straight stem underneath.

Write a line of Yy:

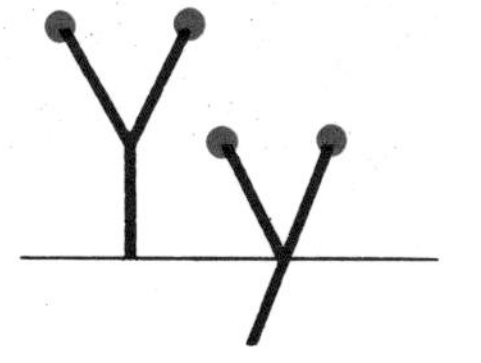

Write and read:
yet yes yam

Now this letter is peculiar. When it is at the beginning of words it says 'y', but when it is at the end it says 'i'.

You know lots of such words—all of two syllables:
funny foggy silly bunny lucky.

And names:
Jimmy Henry Micky.

Write and read:

Yes, his hat is funny.

I had a lucky penny.

Learn these new sight words: you your.

Read them in these sentences and then make up some of your own:

Your dress is pretty.

Your pup is big but your cat is not.

She will see you into the bus, Jimmy.

When 'y' is at the end of words of one syllable it has the long sound of 'i':
my by

abcdefghijklmnopqrstuvwxyz

w

Find this letter on the alphabet chart.

'w' is the sound at the beginning of:
was, water, window, weather, watch, wobble, well, witch, worm, wing.

Look at the pictures and say their names.

Say the sound—'w'.

Hear it in the middle of:
beware awake unwind

The name of 'w' is 'double-U'.

It is very easy to write as we already know how to make 'v' and it is just two 'v's joined together.

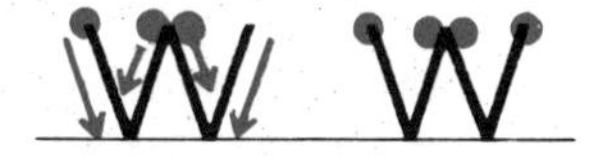

Show templates of 'v' and 'w'.

Follow useful introductory practices.

Write a line of 'w'.
The capital is just the same, but it is a tall letter.

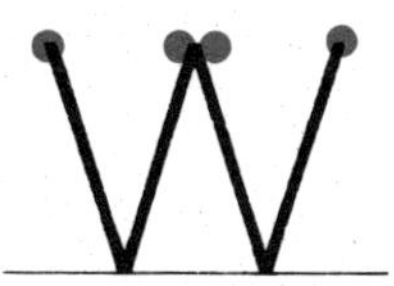

Write a line of both:

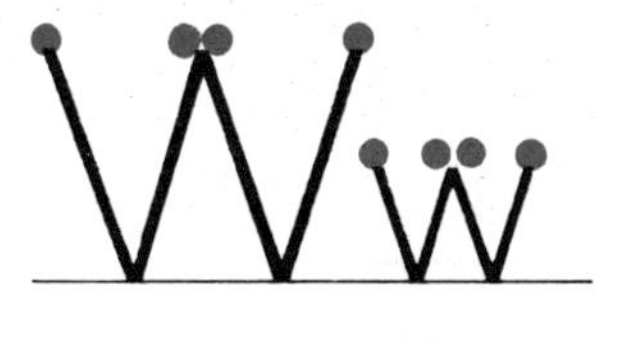

Write and read:

wet wags wig will
Willy was wobbly.
Willy had a wobbly wig.
Was Willy wobbly?
Yes, he was.

Illustrate with hand puppet.

Teach Wee Willy Winky nursery rhyme, either from a book if one child is being taught, or from a wall chart clearly written out for a class.

REVISION AND GAMES

Let's have some more games.

Does this make sense?
_ucky _ulu _icked a _olly.

What letter would you need to fill in the spaces to make the sentence make sense?

Write the sentence and then read it.

What letter do you need to make this sentence make sense?
Mumm_ and Dadd_ had a funn_ pupp_.

Do you remember the vowels clearly?

Revise the sounds of: a e i o u

Fill in the spaces with vowels to make words:

t_cks w_ll

t_cks p_ll

t_cks s_ll

D_n _s a f_ssy d_g.

I c_n sk_p _nd j_mp.

L_t _s g_ _nd h_ve a c_p _f m_lk.

Make puzzles for each other by writing lists of words with particular letters missed out.

How many words can you make from:
w t e g m a

Draw and label:
a cat in a hat
a pig in a wig
a pet in a net
a hen in a pen
a silly rat in a frilly hat.

Make lists of words that rhyme with
rat men mill pin fan

Make words out of these jumbled letters:

bew

tma

sey

nru

das

gol

shi

Make as many words as you can by adding letters to these beginnings:

hu_ ne_ ha_ mo_ bi_

ca_ ge_ nu_ ru_ sa_

Teachers and parents can make up many more games such as these, written out on cards, and children can take them to use as needed or as a privilege or reward for other work well done.

abcdefghijklmnopqrstuvwxyz

Another letter made out of sloping lines is 'x'. It is not found in many words. Its sound is like 'ks'.

It is in the middle of:
exit.

Find it on the alphabet chart.

You can hear it at the end of:
fox box mix axe

Look at the pictures and say their names, listening carefully to the sound on the end of the words.

Its name is 'ex'.

Make a sloping line from left to right and cross over it with another sloping line coming from right to left. The trick is to make the lines cross in the middle and not to make the letter too thin or too fat.

Write a line of these:

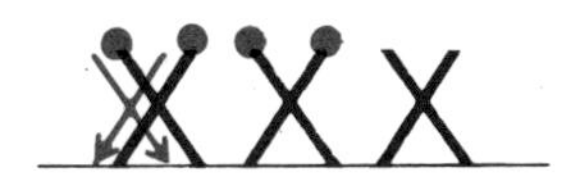

Go through useful practices.
The capital is just the same, but tall:

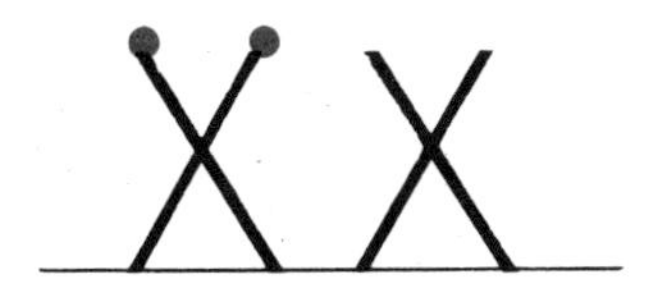

Make a line of both:

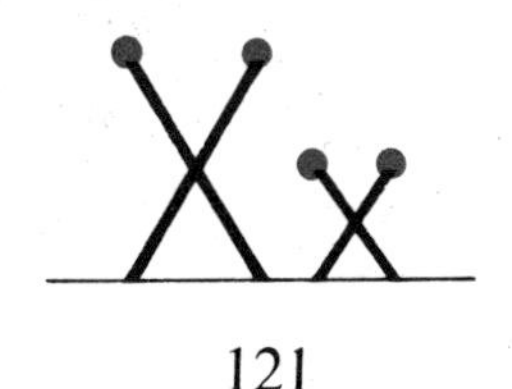

Write and read:

fox box mix fix

We will fix the top of the box.

You can mix the pins in a box.

You will often see Christmas shortened and written 'Xmas' but this does not sound the 'x' sound.

MORE SIGHT WORDS

Now we have another sight word: are

We are hot.
You are not.

Have fun putting these words into sentences with 'are':
funny lucky cats dogs

Like this:

Cats are lucky.

Learn these as sight words:

here **there**

Now make sentences using these words as well. Here is one:

There are lots of lucky cats here.

Make sentences choosing some words from these lists in this order:

There **Here**	**are**	**lots of**	**funny** **silly** **fat** **white**	**ducks** **hens**	**here** **there**

Make more cards of this kind, offering a choice of word combinations, to give practice in sentence structure.

abcdefghijklmnopqrstuvwxyz

z

z is the last letter in the alphabet so it is easily found on the alphabet chart. Find it.

It is the first sound in:
zoo, zebra, zoom, zero, zig-zag, zip.

Look at the pictures and say their names.

Say the sound—'z'.

It is the last sound in:
buzz, fuzz, fizz, size.

Hear it in the middle of:
amazing, dazed.

Its name is 'zed'.

We write it by making a straight line across the top, a sloping line right to left, and a straight line back, just the same size as the top line, and exactly underneath it. It will fit into a little box drawn between the lines.

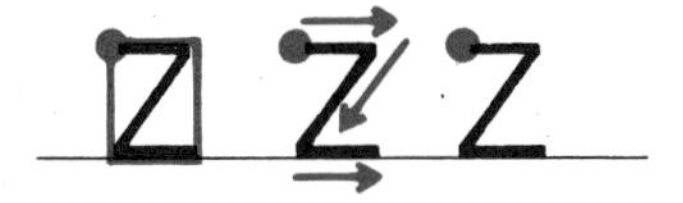

Write a line of 'z'.

The capital is just the same, but tall: Z

Write a row of both: Z z

Write and read: zoo fuzz fizz
There is a buzz in the zoo.
Zebras go into zoos.
A tip top fuzzy wuzzy will buzz and hum.

abcdefghijklmnopqrstuvwxyz

Now we come to a queer consonant.

Find it on the alphabet chart.

It is the only one we have yet to learn. Its sound is like 'kw'.

You can hear it in:
queer, quack, quick, quality, quantity, queen, quilt

Look at the pictures and say their names.

Say the sound—'q'.

Listen to it in these words and say them, listening to your voice:
queen, square, squeeze, sequin, squeak,

Its name is 'kew'.

Show templates of o, a, l, q.

To write it, make an 'o' and then make it into an 'a' and keep on going down to make a tail, giving it a little flick at the bottom.

Follow the usual practices.

Write a line of 'q'.

Capital Q also starts as a capital O and it has a little graceful tail along the line:

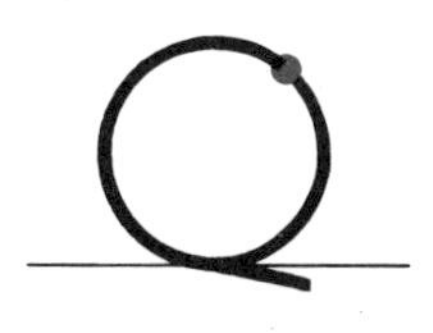

Write a line of both:

Qq

'q' never stands on its own. It is always followed by 'u'. Both letters make just one sound, 'kw'.

Write a line of:

qu qu

Write and read:

quack quick quill

Ducks quack quickly.

DAILY PRACTICES

Now all the vowels and consonants have been presented. When the sounds of all the letters are established, see that the names are known, clear and distinct from the sounds. Reinforce the knowledge of the names and sounds of letters with practices, games and competitions until they are recognized quickly and without error.

Daily practice of the following will speed and reinforce understanding of reading and writing:

Sounds of letters from the alphabet chart.
Names of letters from the alphabet chart.
Flash cards of sight words and frequently used words.

Emphasise that the *first letter* of a word is the one to be *sounded first* as it leads to the sound of the whole word. Get the child to 'read' any book, pointing to and sounding the first letter only of each word. When blends and digraphs are taught this may be adjusted accordingly.

Read nursery rhymes, favourite songs and jingles aloud together from charts.

Make a collection on big pieces of paper of sentences the children have written. Read these over together, getting the children to copy your intonation, fluency and naturalness.

Do not accept stilted, single-word reading for long. Get recognition of groups of words and phrases:

on the mat
up the hill
at the top
up we go
there you are

so that they are read fluently and naturally, just as in ordinary speech. Make a large collection of these and have them available on a page or chart.

The way is now open for the child to write simple sentences, *understanding what he is doing*, and this must be generously encouraged. Particular topics can be followed up and expanded into individual or class 'books' that all can help to write, read and illustrate, each contributing at his own level.

NEXT STEPS

The concepts presented in this book provide a basis from which further instruction in reading can proceed. This will include the sounds of letters grouped together in diphthongs (ea, ai, ow, etc.) and digraphs (sl, gr, tr, etc.) and common beginnings and endings (in-, un-, dis-, ex-; -ful, -less, -ing, etc.). The new ideas will be more readily understood if there is complete confidence in the simple sounds so far used. At the same time the vocabulary of sight words may be quickly expanded in response to the child's interests. The knowledge of sounds and letters already given will have established a basis of understanding of why words say what they do.

GAMES & ACTIVITIES

Pages on which games and activities already occur are 24, 30, 37, 40, 67, 118, 119 and 123. Here are some further suggestions.

To strengthen the habit of listening, it is a good idea to develop the practice of giving the instructions to be followed *just once.*

Most of the following games will serve to sharpen perception and memory.

Short Vowel Snap

Take 25 cards, playing card size, or about 5 cm × 8 cm for smaller children. Allow five cards for each vowel. On three of them write the letter, varying the size and colour. On the remaining two draw pictures of objects beginning with that sound. Be certain the *sound* is right: e.g. apple and arrow, but not aunt or apron.

Shuffle the cards. Divide the pack in half and let each player hold his cards face downwards. The first player places one card face up on the table and *says clearly the short sound of the letter* or the short sound of the vowel at the beginning of the name of the object. The second player places a card beside it and says the sound shown. Play continues with each player placing a card on his own pile and saying the appropriate sound until the top cards on each pile show a similar sound. The first player to say 'Snap' wins both piles of cards and adds them underneath those in his hand. He then starts again and play continues until one player wins all the cards.

This game is very popular and excellent for remedial work. The principle can be applied to any letter or sound needing practice.

Word Magic

Can you change a dog into a cat?

Write *dog* and under it write another word, changing one letter only. Write another word under that, again changing one letter only, and carry on until *cat* can be produced:

dog
dot
cot
cat

Can you change a *pig* into a *rat*?
a *peg* into a *pin*?
a *pot* into a *pan*?
a *bus* into a *van*?
a *hen* into a *fox*?
sun into *fog*?

I Spy

Caller says: 'I spy
With my little eye
Something beginning with (for example) "t".'

The one who guesses the object the caller has in mind, has the next turn.

Catch the Letter

Call out words and get children to write down initial letters, or middle letters, or last letters.

Catch the Number

Let one person clap, ring, bounce or skip while the others write down the number of times it is done.

How Many?

Have one person call a number and others write it down. Then call two numbers, and then groups of numbers, until they are quite complex.
The same can be done with letters.

Common Sounds

Listen for the common sound in:
catch, caterpillar, can, canopy
dog, dot, dolly

Team Listening Game

Divide the class into teams. Whisper the same sentence to each team leader. He whispers it to the next child, and so on down the line until the last child brings it back to the teacher. See which team can give it back accurately.

Progressive Memory Games

The Tea Game: Children sit in a circle.
1st child: Last night I had fish for tea.
2nd child: Last night I had fish and cake for tea.
3rd child: Last night I had fish and cake and sausages for tea, etc.
Competitor drops out if he cannot remember the sequence, and the game progresses until there is only one person left.

There are many variations on this:

The Holiday Game:

1st child: I am going to Austria for the holidays.
2nd child: I am going to Austria and Brighton for the holidays.
3rd child: I am going to Austria and Brighton and New York for the holidays, etc.

The Clothes Game

1st child: Yesterday I wore a cardigan.
2nd child: Yesterday I wore a cardigan and yellow socks.
3rd child: Yesterday I wore a cardigan and yellow socks and two red ribbons, etc.

Clapping Game

The first child claps twice and says,
'I clapped twice'.
2nd child claps five times and says,
'George clapped twice, and I clapped five times' etc.

A Looking Game: Kim's Game

Place several familiar objects on a tray—a knife, to match, an orange, etc.
Show them to the children for a few moments, then cover the tray and see who can remember what was on it.

Variations

Feel objects inside a stocking on cloth bag and remember what they were.

Flash Letters

Holding up cards with hand puppets makes it fun for small children.
Hold up a card showing a letter.
Let the children write the letter.
Hold up another letter.
Let the children write it.
And so on. Encourage the children to try to make a word from their letters.
The first to make a word gets a point.
The same can be done with words to be made into sentences.

Filling in the Gaps

Make up a story, leaving out certain words. When you speak the story, hold up cards which spell the missing word. Get children to say or write the word. For example, have ready cards showing 'I', 'cup', 'to' and 'milk'. Then say: Last night when . . . (hold up card for 'I') had a . . . ('cup') of tea I forgot . . . ('to') put in the . . . ('milk').

This game can have a written form. Have cards of sentences with missing words. These are written in any order at the bottom of the card and have to be selected. Children write out the complete sentence.

Example: Let . . . see if it . . . your . . .
hat is me

Make little words from big words or from letters being currently studied.

Books of word games, join-the-dots games and puzzles of all kinds can be purchased inexpensively. Separate the pages and store them in a box from which children can help themselves as a privilege for work well done, rainy lunchtimes, etc. Have boards or thick card with bull-dog clips and a supply of tracing paper, so that the same pages can be used many times.

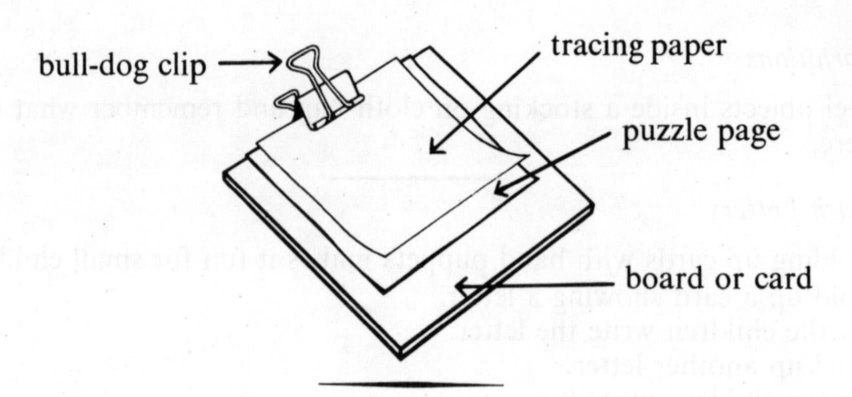

Crosswords

Buy the cheap little books available, separate the pages, and use as above.

Word Bits

Write out the first bi-syllabic words:

into, upon, etc.

Cut them in half and get the children to reassemble them.
Make sentences including these words.

Make a frieze of the letter being studied.

Let the children make, for instance, a big 'g', a little 'g', various coloured 'g's, pictures of things beginning with 'g', in crayon, chalk, pencil, ink, paint. Add cut-outs of rough and smooth paper.

Mark out several of the letters being studied in large clear forms on the floor or playground, using chalk. Call out one of the letters and have individual children or team members run to touch the letter called.

Make big letters on paper and pin these on various children's jerseys. Call out the children and get them to stand in order. Other children write and read the word spelt.

Place in the Alphabet

At first find the approximate place by asking: Is it near the beginning, in the middle, or near the end of the alphabet? Then become more and more precise, and ask which letter follows which.

For example: 'Where is "b"?'
'Where is "z"?'
'Where is "t"?'

'What is the letter before/after "g"?'
'Where shall we look for "m"?'
'Where shall we look for the letter at the beginning of "happy"?'

AIDS

Some simple aids will help with following the instructions given in the text. Printed at the back of the book you will find:

Flash cards of the first sight words.
Pages of letters and objects for matching.
Designs for templates of letters.
A chart of the days of the week.
Chart of numbers.
A chart of colours.

The letter templates can be made of wood or of thick card cut from the designs printed on pages 153–7. Colour the vowels red and the consonants blue.

Accuracy in size and shape is essential.

These letter shapes are of great value for analysing the structure of letters, for feeling with the fingers, for tracing round, for making rubbings. They are indispensable for partially sighted children.

Sandpaper letters: Paint with a ½″ brush in pale colour on sandpaper and cut out.
Mount on thick card.
Otherwise use templates described above, traced on to sandpaper.

Write mirror letters and words on the back of a piece of paper with a dressmaker's tracing wheel, pushing through the paper on to a soft substance underneath. When the paper is turned over children can run their fingers round and feel the shapes.

Pictures and letters can be stuck on to charts for the wall and odd moments can be used for revision.

Cover the bottom of a shallow baking tin (20 cm × 25 cm) with fine dry sand. Children love to practise writing letter shapes in this with their fingers. If the bottom of the tin is enamelled in a bright colour it is more fun and the letters show through more clearly.

Make stands for assembling letters or words from firm cardboard. For letter-stand measure card 16 cm × 20 cm. Fold lengthwise at 6 cm and 12 cm. Staple securely at ends.

For words-stand cut card 16 cm × 40 cm.

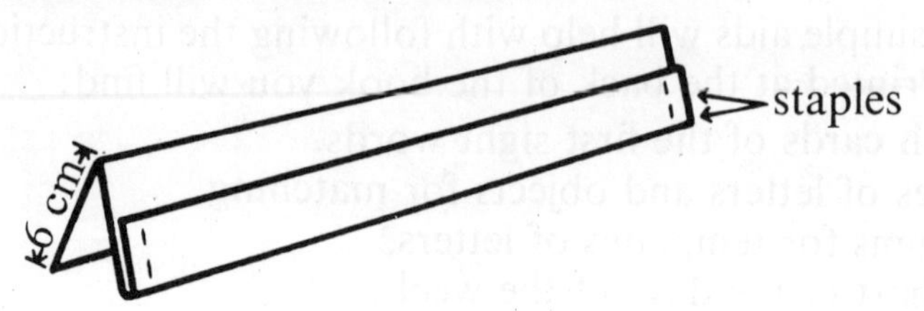

Into these stands can be slotted letters for making words, and words for making sentences.

Make letter cards 10 cm × 5 cm.

Make word cards 10 cm × width appropriate to length of word.

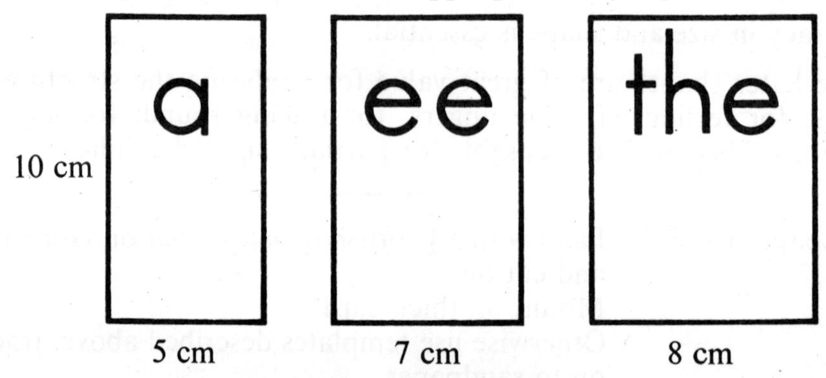

This equipment is valuable in various ways:

1. For the teacher to use to demonstrate

(a) how a word is built up, as on page 47 and later.

(b) quick interchange of vowel or consonant to give different words, e.g. put 'p' and 't' in position at beginning and end of stand, and all vowels in the middle. Quickly change vowel in the middle, getting children to read words; pit, pat, pet, pot.

(c) Interchange of words, e.g. *a* dog, *the* dog.

2. For children to use to build words, phrases or sentences which they can then copy into their books.

Mount the pictures and letters printed on pp. 143–151 on cardboard. Parents could help make individual sets of these for the child to use at home and bring to school to use. Colour the pictures.

At first children can match just the lower case letter and the picture; next match capital and lower case letter and picture; or just capital and lower case letter.

The teacher or a child can hold up a picture—children write down the letter or hold up their own letter.

Peg letters on to a clothes line to make words:

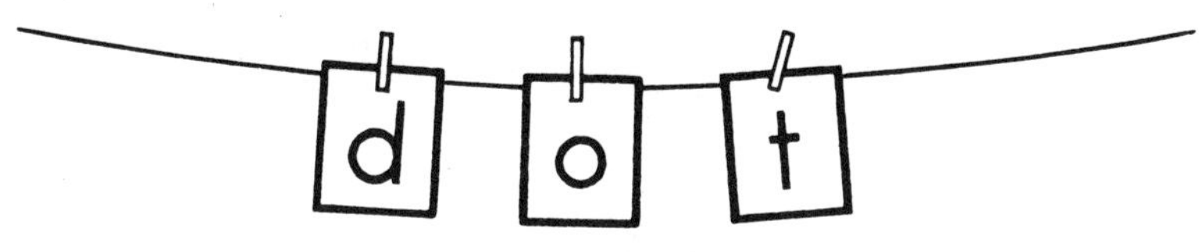

Make a set of blank flash cards the same size as that printed on page 39 to fill in with sight and interest words as these occur.

Make sentence cards as words become known. For example:

I We	are is was am	here coming	to at up	the dog the back the hill

I He	had am has	a the	cat cup boy

Encourage the child to see how many sentences he can make from different combinations of words.

Introduce words of current interest also on these cards.

If your group is not too large a wall chart can be kept to record the best letters written by each child.

Cut them out and paste on the chart. Insist on an excellent standard before a letter is added, a privilege to be worked for. If you do not want to cut work out, shade in the appropriate square:

	a	b	c	d	e	f	g	h
Anna						f		
Henry		b						h
Greg				d				h

Make a spinner of the shape shown with different letter combinations on each side. Push a sharpened match through the centre. Take turns to spin and at each stop everyone writes down the letter touching the table. First to make a word gets a point.

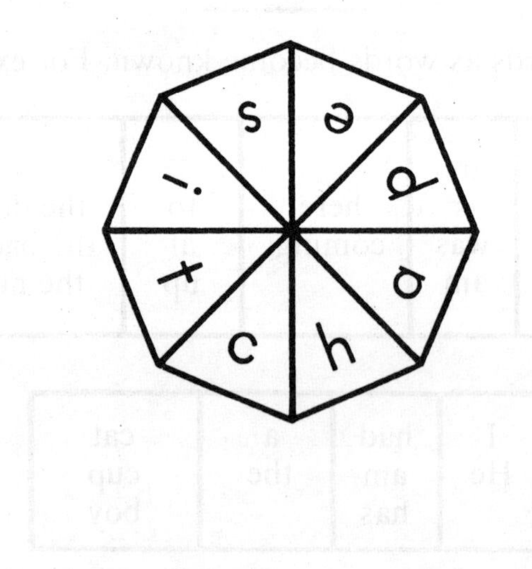

the	**the cat**	**the**
and	**the cat and the dog**	**and**
at	**the cat is at the top**	**at**
come	**Come on.**	**come**
to	**Tell it to come.**	**to**
I	**I can come.**	**I**
was	**The tap was on.**	**was**
a	**Can it run up a hill?**	**a**
is	**The pup is a pet.**	**is**
see	**The dog can see the cat.**	**see**
in	**Come in.**	**in**
will	**The pup will get in.**	**will**
be	**Will he be up?**	**be**
me	**Come to me.**	**me**
she	**She can see the sun.**	**she**
of	**Get a cup of milk.**	**of**
off	**Get off.**	**off**
for	**Cut it up for him.**	**for**
as	**Can you hop as well as you jump?**	**as**
if	**Come if you can.**	**if**
but	**Your dog is fat but your cat is not.**	**but**
from	**It is from me.**	**from**
have	**I have the mugs.**	**have**
you	**Will you have it?**	**you**
your	**Your van is red.**	**your**
it	**Can you get it?**	**it**
are	**Your cats are fat.**	**are**
here	**Is he here yet?**	**here**
there	**His hat is there.**	**there**
on	**He sat on it.**	**on**
am	**I am here.**	**am**
up	**There it is up there.**	**up**
go	**Will it go in there?**	**go**
no	**No, it will not.**	**no**
has	**He has to go.**	**has**
we	**We can skip.**	**we**
us	**Can you see us?**	**us**
cannot	**He cannot get in there.**	**cannot**
into	**I can let you into the hut.**	**into**
until	**Go on until you are at the end.**	**until**

FLASH CARDS

Copy the examples of flash cards on the opposite page or paste the page on cardboard and cut along the lines.

the	and
at	come
to	I
was	a
is	see

LETTERS AND OBJECTS FOR MATCHING

See pages 23 and 136 for the way in which the letters and objects below are intended to be used. Do not use the capital letters until they have been introduced in the text.

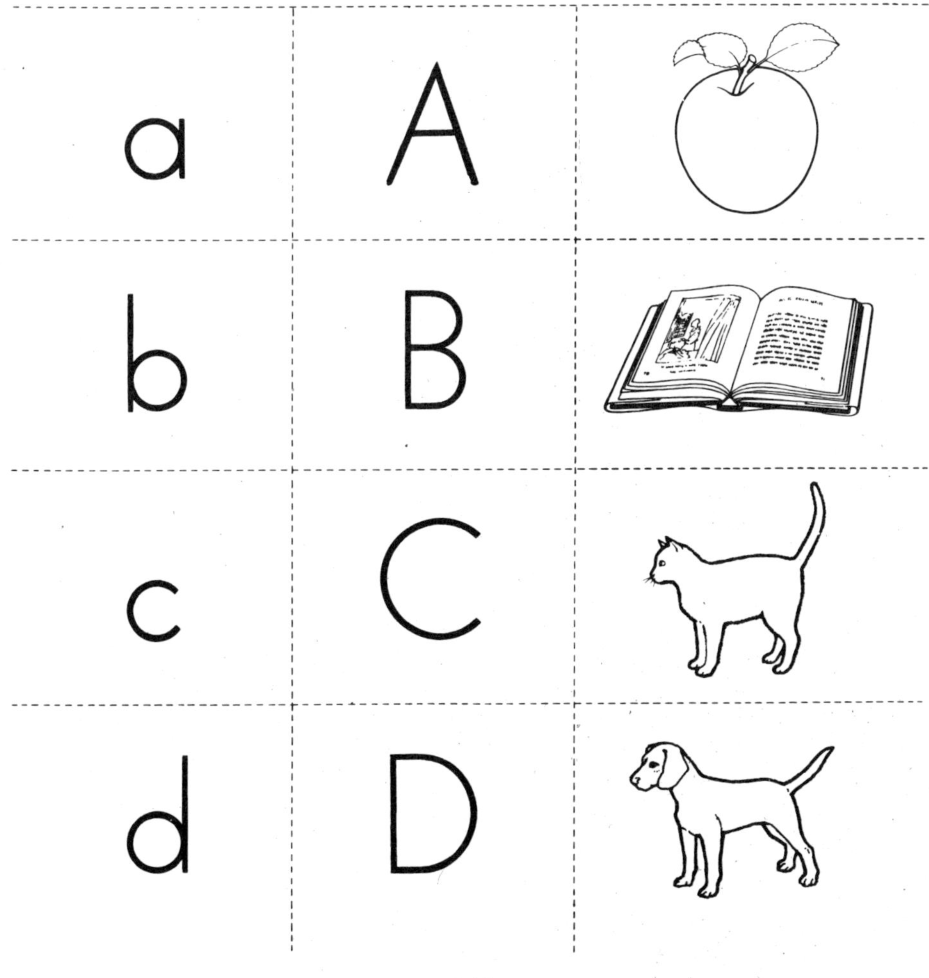

e	E	
f	F	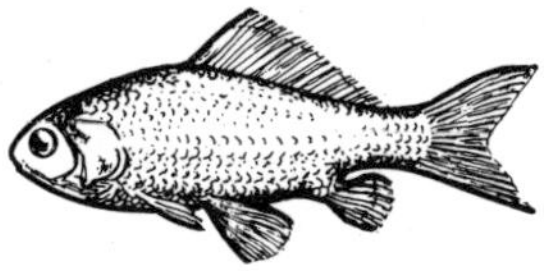
g	G	
h	H	
i	I	
j	J	

k	K	
l	L	
m	M	
n	N	
o	O	
p	P	

q	Q	
r	R	
s	S	
t	T	
u	U	
v	V	

w W
x X
y Y
z Z

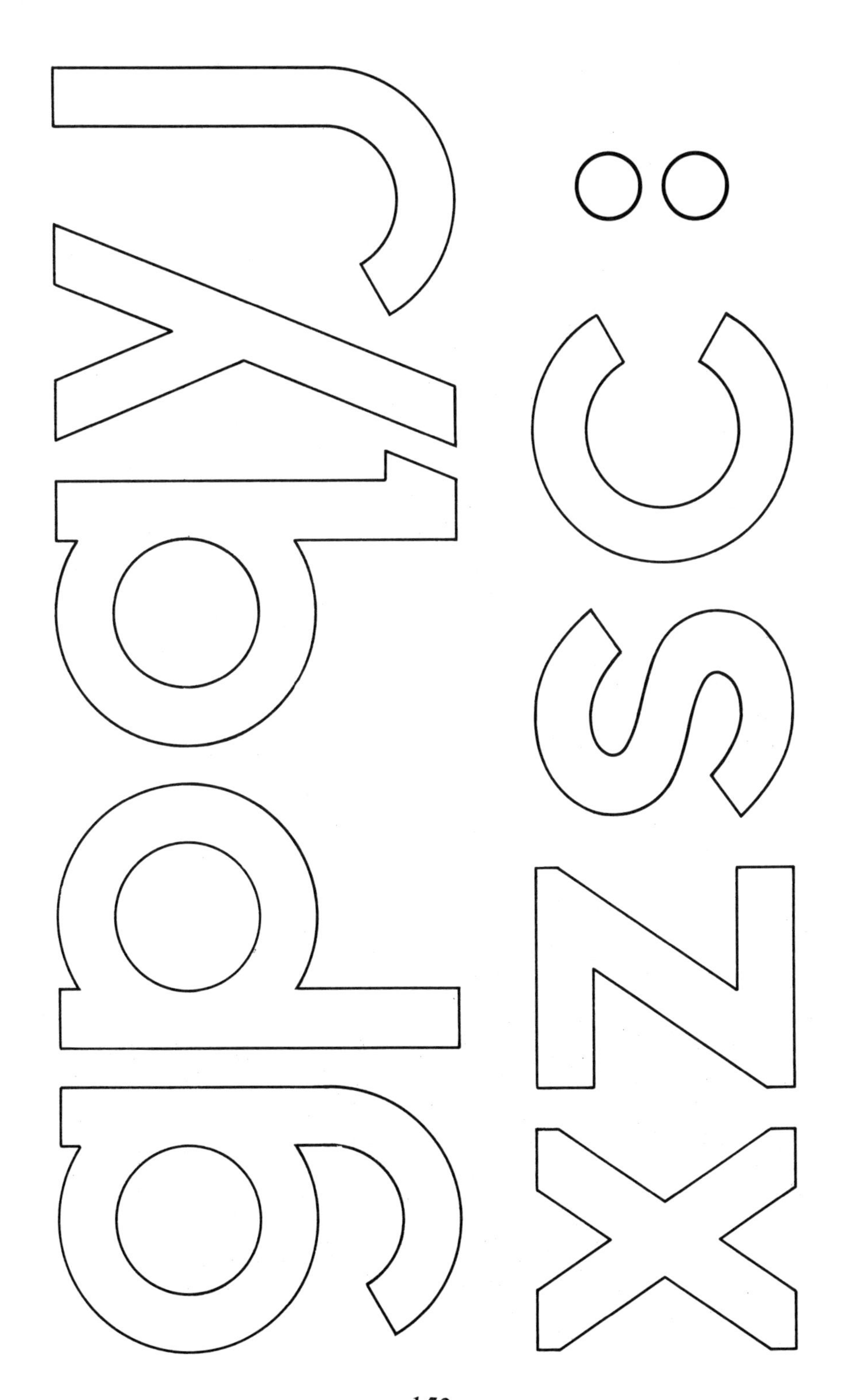

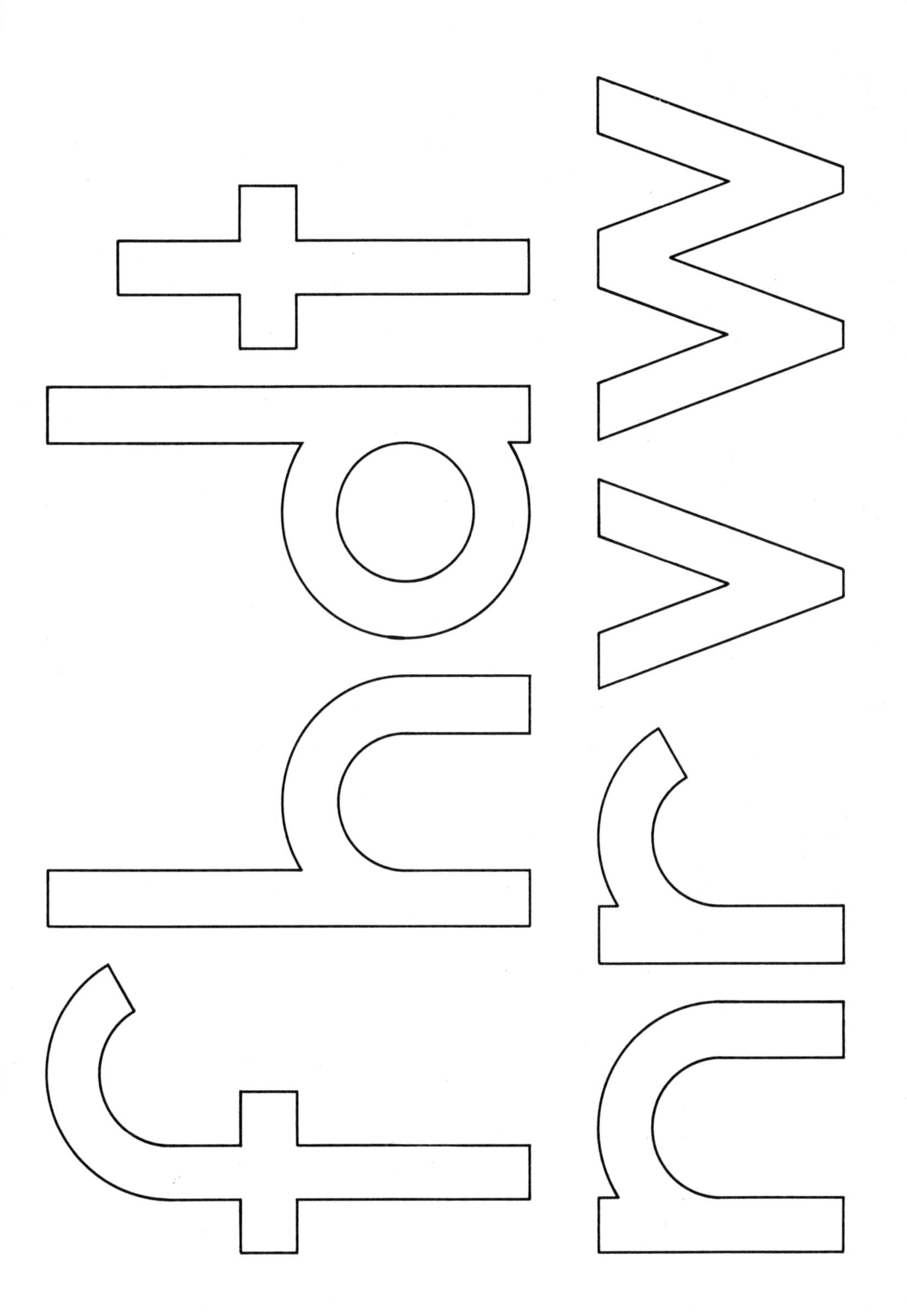

DAYS of the WEEK

Sunday

Monday

Tuesday

Wednesday

Thursday

Friday

Saturday

NUMBERS

1	one
2	two
3	three
4	four
5	five
6	six
7	seven
8	eight
9	nine
10	ten

COLOURS

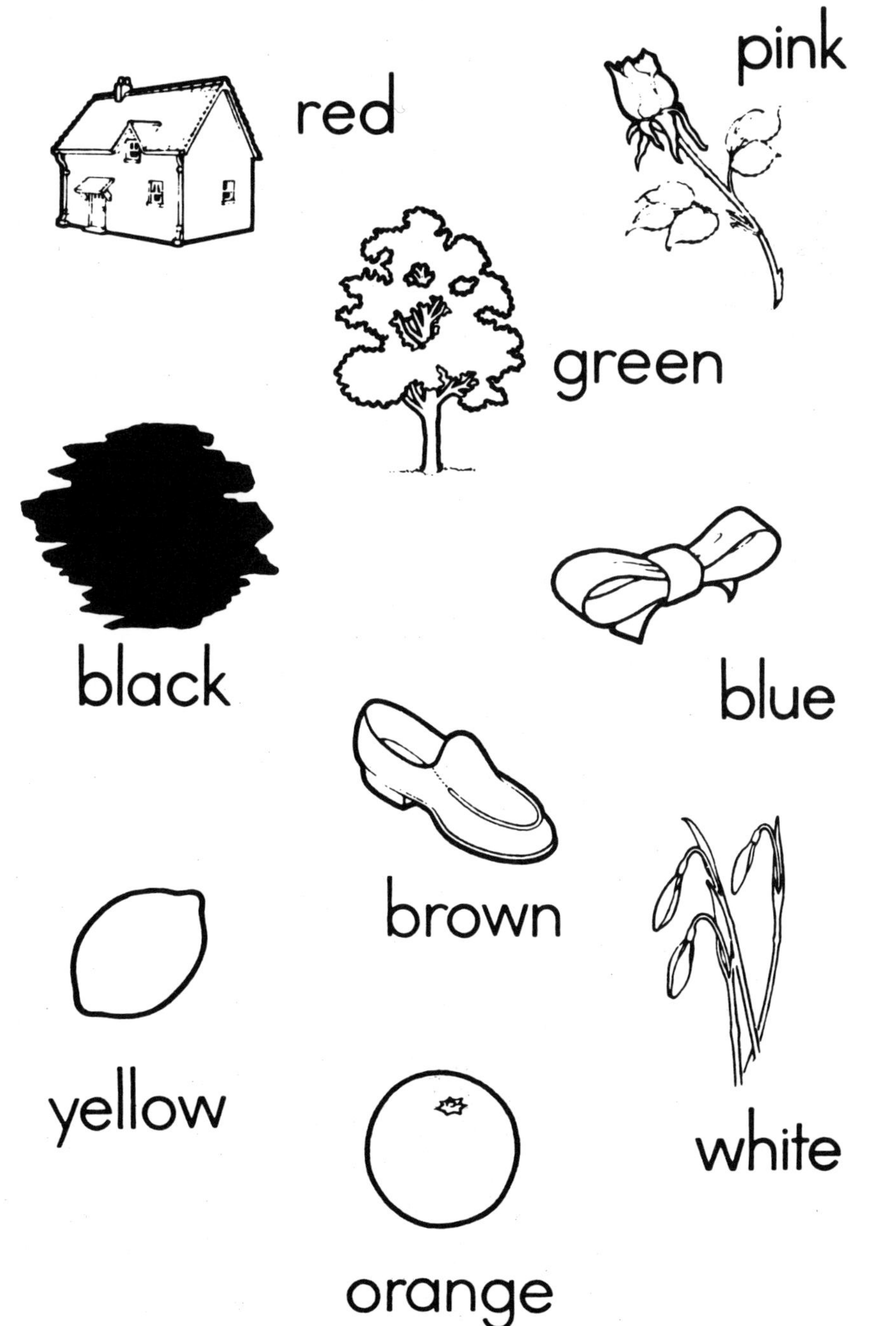

Colour in pictures carefully with bold, clear colours.